SERIOUSLY FUNNY 2

SERIOUSLY FUNNY 2

**More musings between two good friends
on life, love and God**

Adrian Plass and
Jeff Lucas

Authentic

Copyright © 2012 Adrian Plass and Jeff Lucas

18 17 16 15 14 13 12   7 6 5 4 3 2 1

First published 2012 by Authentic Media Limited
52 Presley Way, Crownhill, Milton Keynes, MK8 0ES.
www.authenticmedia.co.uk

The right of Adrian Plass and Jeff Lucas to be identified as the Authors
of this Work has been asserted by them in accordance with the
Copyright, Designs and Patents Act 1988.

British Library Cataloguing in Publication Data

A catalogue record for this book is available from the British Library.

978-1-85078-967-3

Unless otherwise stated Scripture quotations are taken from the
HOLY BIBLE, NEW INTERNATIONAL VERSION. Copyright ©
1979, 1984 by Biblica. Used by permission of Hodder & Stoughton
Publishers, a member of the Hachette Livre UK Group. All rights
reserved.
Scripture taken from THE MESSAGE. Copyright © 1993, 1994, 1995,
1996, 2000, 2001, 2002. Used by permission of NavPress
Publishing Group.

Cover Design by David Smart
Printed and bound in Great Britain by CPI Group (UK) Ltd.,
Croydon, CR0 4YY.

Dedications

Adrian: To Sheridan and Merryn, who understand what resurrection really means.

Jeff: To Adrian and Pauline. Thanks for four decades of friendship with Kay and me. Pauline, you've never left us in any doubt that you love us. And Adrian, thanks for asking interminable questions way before questions were cool.

Introduction: Adrian

Dear Jeff,

I'm glad we started writing to each other again. We both lead such busy lives, and you spend half your time on aeroplanes trying to work out whether you're on your way to England or on the way back. I'm happy about us finding this time to correspond for at least three reasons.

The first is that I enjoy laughing a lot and crying a little, and your letters are very good at making that happen. We are both incurably anecdotal, and I know that you are no more anxious to find a cure for that condition than I am. What do you think, Jeff? Do more interesting and amusing things happen to us than other people, or is it just we are quicker to notice them and make little notes on the backs of envelopes, in case we want to 'use' them one day? Either way, I do love your stories, and I hope you sometimes enjoy mine. By the way, we must sit down one wet Saturday morning and exchange embroidery tips and techniques.

Secondly, there is something about the very nature of letters that makes it possible to explore dangerous things in a safe place. I don't decry appropriate restraint, of course, but I do think I'm beginning to learn that blandness can be as evil and disempowering as excess. The fact that we own and air our questions and complications is, I hope, a mark and an acknowledgement of the freedom that is God's generous gift to those who want to follow Jesus rather than learn how to be a Christian, whatever that means. Yes, we take care, but care is by no means always synonymous with caution, and thank God for that, I say.

My third point is that, in some of the letters written since our first co-written book *Seriously Funny* came out, I think we have communicated in a more directly responsive way to each other. We now know these exchanges are going to be published as a follow-up, with the inventive title *Seriously Funny 2*, but there is very little of the content that I would want to change *pour encourager* or indeed to protect any of *les autres* who might get round to reading them. I detect in the second half of our correspondence in particular, written in a relatively short space of time, a new intensity and a fresh commitment to personal revelation. This is a risky business naturally, but I believe the risks involved are well worth taking. Perhaps the bottom line is that Jesus never minded anyone asking questions, as long as they didn't mind hearing the answers. And that usually leads to a choice. His way, or the broad highway?

See you soon I hope, Jeff.

    Love,

        Adrian

Introduction: Jeff

Dear Adrian,

I'm glad we decided to write again too, and not just because some people will be able to take a peek at our letters because they buy the book, and hopefully be cheered up/encouraged/provoked/comforted (delete as applicable, though I'm hoping for all four).

And I agree: letter writing is good, because it allows us to separate what are often conjoined twins in the church: questions and answers. Sometimes it seems that whenever someone dares to pose a question in the church, someone else immediately slams their foot on the certainty accelerator and hurtles themselves forward with a sure, solid answer. But questions need to percolate, don't they? Jesus knew that, and so spent three years with his friends, not only steering them through some jaw-dropping miracles, but also scattering question marks along the way as they pondered those pithy, colourful parables. The best questions wriggle under our skin, gnaw away at our hearts, and sometimes (maddeningly) keep us staring desperately through the gloom at our bedroom ceilings, as question-fuelled insomnia deprives us from rest. And that's why I like writing this way, Adrian, although there will be some challenges. After all, some of our letters were exchanged with me, bleary-eyed, parked at my desk in Colorado at 4 a.m., while, in a time zone seven hours ahead, you tapped away at your laptop at a more respectable time (yes, I'm so much more committed than you).

By the way, I'd really like to give you (and our readers) the impression that I chortled knowingly at your inclusion of a couple of French terms, but the truth is that I didn't have a clue what you were talking about when you mentioned *les autres* and *pour encourager*. I am sitting on a train writing this, and tried saying them out loud to give myself a hint, leading other passengers to think that I am perhaps a reincarnation of Inspector Clouseau.

So please, be a good chap, and translate for *moi, s'il vous plait*?

> Much love,
> Jeff

PS: You mentioned swopping embroidery tips. I once read a fabulous book on quilting (seriously, I did) written by someone who visited an Amish community in the USA and was moved by the simplicity and symmetry of their quilting. Sometimes I wish life was like that, Adrian, all bold squares and perfectly lined up stitches. But it's not that way, is it? Hence these letters . . .

Dear Jeff,

Cordon bleu! Cordon bleu! I've had to look it up now, blow you! Apparently *Pour encourager les autres* means 'to encourage the others', but it clearly doesn't work, so *les autres* can jolly well *encourage* themselves from now on. Can't a humble writer indulge in a little affectation just occasionally? *A la carte!* Life is not half as *en suite* as we might wish sometimes . . .

> Talk soon, Adrian

ONE

Dear Jeff,

It seems an age since our first tour together. What a great time that was. Considering the fact that we got up on stage each night without any clear idea of where our conversation was going or what was likely to happen, I think it turned out pretty well. So much laughter, and, ironically perhaps, so much pain as well. Some of the people who came along had really been through it. Do you remember us saying that the picture we were getting of the Christian church was more like a battlefield after the conflict than anything else? Wounds and tears and a wild yearning for home. How do you staunch the bleeding of so many broken hearts? No easy answers to that, but we won't give up, will we? Not until God does, and as he never will, I guess we're in it for the long haul. I'm glad. I want to be part of it, and I know you do as well.

Anyway, the thing that prompted me to write was something that happened the other day. As you will remember, quite a lot of the stories we told in the course of our tour were accounts of how utterly ridiculous you and I manage to be from time to time. A couple of weeks ago two face-reddening experiences happened to me in two consecutive days. A record, even for my good self.

The first was on a Monday afternoon, when folk were arriving at Scargill Conference Centre (the place in Yorkshire where Bridget and I are based at present) for a teaching week. Because the person who organised this event suffers dreadfully from the infectious Anglican disease of alliteration, the course was entitled *Leaders Learning to Listen*. I wasn't actually involved in the programme, but I happened to be around as people turned up, so I thought I might as well practise a bit of warm welcoming. When I noticed an elderly gentleman coming through the front door and hovering slightly nervously by the reception window, I decided to swing into action.

'Hello!' I said, stepping forward and beaming brightly. 'Great to see you! You must be here for *Leaders Learning to Listen*.'

The elderly man leaned forward, cupped a hand around his right ear, and said, 'Eh?'

I guffawed with charitably disproportionate enthusiasm, and then clapped him on the back and said, 'Ah, good one! Yes, very funny,' and to keep the flow of innocent merriment going even longer, I cupped my hand behind my ear just as he had done. My new acquaintance didn't seem to find this very funny. He didn't even smile. Raising his hand to his ear once more, he again enquired, 'Eh?'

A cold hand gripped my heart.

Yes, you guessed it. He hadn't come for *Leaders Learning to Listen*, and he had cupped his hand behind his ear because he was profoundly deaf and had left his hearing-aid at home. You couldn't make it up, could you? My subsequent burbling attempt to explain why I had not only appeared to find evidence of his deafness screamingly funny, but had actually mocked his affliction by mimicking his hand actions, was not wholly successful.

In fact, it was like trying to unpick a kite string that has become hopelessly, impenetrably tangled. Oh dear.

The second incident was equally ridiculous, but it offers one or two interesting implications. My wife had received a phone call from someone called Mavis. Mavis was deeply distressed and wondered if it was possible to come and have a chat with Bridget for an hour or so. Later that day a message was passed to me saying that Mavis had arrived a little early, and asking if I could look after her for a few minutes until Bridget was free. Hurrying down to the reception area, I discovered a surprisingly clear-eyed and attractive young lady waiting in the Sun Lounge. Oh, well, I thought, appearances can be very deceptive. She looks fine, but who knows what turmoil is going on under the surface? I must be very gentle and caring.

'You must be Mavis,' I murmured therapeutically.

'Yes,' she answered, with a tinge of unease that I judged to be totally understandable.

'Well, I'm Adrian, and Bridget's already seen you?'

'Er, yes – yes, she has.'

'And she's going to see you in a few minutes? That's right, isn't it?'

'That's what she said,' replied Mavis.

If I hadn't been so busy trying not to alarm the poor girl I might have noticed that the haunted expression in her eyes was that of someone who has wandered into an asylum by mistake and is looking for the nearest exit.

'Well,' I coaxed, 'shall we sit down for a few minutes at one of these tables until she's free? Would that be a good idea?'

Hearing Bridget calling my name urgently from the door of the reception office at that moment, I excused myself and walked over to see what she wanted.

'It's the wrong Mavis!' she hissed. 'Apparently that girl's just come with someone to deliver something, and I've told her I'm going to come and speak to her in a few minutes. The right Mavis has just phoned to say that she's going to be a bit late.'

You couldn't invent that one either, could you? This girl turns up to deliver something or other, and is greeted by two people who magically and inexplicably know what her name is, treat her as though she's made of the finest and most fragile bone china, and announce that she is going to be 'spoken to' if she could just wait a few minutes. What on earth did she make of it all? Quite understandably she left fairly briskly at that point, so we never did have the chance to explain. What are the odds against two women called Mavis popping up at the same time? Must be enormous, Jeff. Wish I'd had a few quid on.

Ludicrous as that situation was, it did make me think about the tone of voice we use when we encounter people here. One of the promises that we community members make is to do our best to treat all guests as we would treat Jesus himself. Not one is to be more or less special than any other. Maybe they should all get the 'Mavis' treatment, preferably without scaring them half to death.

One final thing. Bridget and I led a group for Holy Week this year. On Good Friday we carried a big old cross up to the chapel and laid it on the floor in front of the altar. Lots of us sat or knelt around the cross, just touching it gently, noticing where his feet and his hands and his head would have been. That cross looked so vulnerable splayed out there, so abandoned and hurt. Quite unbidden, a little boy who was part of the group gathered some cushions and placed them gently under the parts of the cross where he thought most of the pain must have been. It was one of the most beautiful things I've ever seen. 'Unless you become like one of these . . .' Too right.

How are things going with you, Jeff? I really would like to know.

Lots of love,
Adrian

TWO

Dear Adrian,

Oh dear. You got yourself in quite a pickle with the poor chap who showed up at the *Leaders Learning to Listen* event minus his hearing aid, didn't you? He must have thought that you were minus your brain. And then you accosted Mavis – the poor girl probably thought you were a kindly, roving pervert. Most of the jams that you and I get ourselves into are either because we haven't actually learned to listen, or we stick our size fifteens into our mouths, because we assume too much.

I try to presume as little as possible these days; when I make a guess, I'm usually wrong. I have a golden rule when meeting any woman who appears to be pregnant. I never comment on her confinement, or ask when the baby is due, even if she seems to be carrying an entire house group in there, and the sound of slightly off-tune guitar strumming is emanating from her gigantic abdomen. The risk is obvious. She might just be fat or, worse still, chronically flatulent. My effusive congratulations on the forthcoming birth might prompt her to slap me if she's just been too long at the McTrough. If trapped wind is the issue, she might suddenly get delivered and blow me to Scunthorpe.

I've also found myself red-faced when assuming a mother-daughter relationship between two women. Bouncing like a pastoral Tigger into a hospital ward, I smiled at the patient and then greeted the lady who stood at the bedside with words that I knew were incendiary as soon as they left my mouth: 'You must be her mother.'

'No', she growled like the child star of *The Exorcist*, 'I'm her sister, and whoever you are, I'll hate you forever.' (Actually, I've never seen *The Exorcist*.) So now I try to make no assumptions, and pause to allow my brain to catch up with my mouth.

There's one exception to this little rule, which I have learned from my friend and colleague Dary Northrop. He is one of the most consistently cheerful chaps I know, and has a PhD in emotional intelligence. When Dary walks into a room full of people, be they known to him or not, he assumes they all like him, until they show him otherwise. That way he's meeting people from a place of security, and doesn't meander around engaging in the vain shadow-boxing that happens when we vaguely suspect others disapprove of us.

Speaking of being liked, you were kind enough to ask how things are with me, and even kinder to add that you really would like to know. Some people politely ask how we're doing, but they're not really looking for an authentic answer, especially if it takes a while. It's awful to launch into a little heart-to-heart, and then notice a vinegary facial expression of acute disinterest.

I blush to confess that I've been guilty of doing this. The *über*-danger zone for feigned interest is Sunday morning, especially when church buildings are thronged with people coming and going, and leaders stride around at speed looking like we definitely have a purpose-driven life. There's a real danger of seeing people, but not really seeing them, if you get my drift.

In America, where I live much of the time, the standard greeting is, 'How you doing?' The expected reply is 'Fine.' In lots of circumstances, this would be a hollow comment.

Hurtling at meteoric speed down the corridor, I had the look of a man with places to go, people to see, issues to sort out: in short, a furrowed-browed leader. Passing by a nondescript looking chap, I smiled pastorally, popped the 'How you doing?' question, and then continued speed walking, without waiting for a response. Stupidly, I obviously thought that just asking was care enough. I got fifty yards down the hall when I heard him yell back 'Fine . . .!' in the style of one of those lederhosen-clad yodellers who appear in yoghurt commercials.

So to answer your kind question, I am fine, mostly. I've just had three weeks of spending far too much time listening to the sound of my own voice. I think that I've preached about 35 times in 21 days. If I have a guardian angel, they are probably in therapy, or perhaps attending an *Angels who are learning to listen even when they're sick of it* conference.

Preaching has a strange psychological effect on me. I mostly love it, sometimes loathe it, but still find the whole exercise a tad confusing. It's a staggering privilege to talk to a group of people with the hope that, somehow, your words might help bring a glimmer of light to them. But then there's the utter absurdity of it all: to think a tiny human could be audacious enough to imagine they could speak for the One who flung the stars into space. At one level, it's a wonderful thought that staggers the imagination. On another, there are times I want to stop preaching forever, and just put the kettle on and tell myself not to be so silly. So I return from these preaching trips with a mixture of gratitude and bewilderment, coupled with the soreness that comes when you've bared the sinfulness and fragility of your soul once again for the edification of the Christian public. You're good at vulnerability, Adrian – do you feel raw after you reveal yet another example of the gift of buffoonery that we both share?

A couple of weeks ago, I was speaking at a conference, and was experiencing that 'I'm a vending machine with a Bible' feeling that speakers get when we dash from seminar to celebration, breathlessly and desperately hoping to be helpful. A lady approached me and, with one short sentence, gave me a gift that I will carry to the grave. 'When you preach, Jeff', she smiled, 'I can breathe.'

I was overwhelmed. We've all fought for air during unrealistic, threatening, or confusing preaching. I've endured a few stifling and claustrophobic sermons. The more the preacher went on, the more frantically my soul thrashed around within me, trying to escape a straitjacket stitched by words. And so the thought that, by God's grace, I might have done something to help someone to breathe was almost too wonderful to believe.

You mentioned the *Seriously Funny* tour that we shared last year. What a mad, wonderful idea it was to go on tour together. There were many memorable moments, but I'd like to mention three of them. Forgive the Trinitarian approach: as a preacher, I wrestle with the temptation to organise all of my thoughts into three or four ideas, begin them with the same letter, close with prayer after I've shared them and then announce the offering. I've obviously been spending way too much time in Christian gatherings.

Back to the tour. I loved the lady who roared with laughter so loudly that she had to run out of the church hall and take cover in the toilet, where she could still be heard howling hysterically. What a magical sound laughter is, don't you think? Whether it's the gentle snigger, the gathering guffaw, or a shoulder-shaking eruption, it's the most gorgeous sound. Then there was the older lady who laughed so much that she had a little accident (actually, that's probably not the best description – it's a bit like describing Niagara Falls as a little waterfall). She utterly and thoroughly wet herself. Not that she admitted it, of course. But her daughter sidled up to me, and with a furtiveness usually associated with the sale of illegal drugs, she whispered, 'That's my Mum over there, and she's totally wet her knickers.'

I was delighted, even if it's a rather unorthodox way of measuring how successful an event has been. Usually Christian speakers count how many people came forward for prayer, or how many hands were raised in response to some invitation, while all the while insisting that of course it doesn't matter how many came forward or raised their hands . . . but underwear wetting could be another criteria for gauging the level of blessing and joy.

'Righto, how many of you have struggled with bladder control at some point during this service? Good. Minor leakage? Lovely. Troublesome mini-tidal event? Wonderful! Full-on soaked-through wettage? God bless you . . .'

But I think my very favourite moment came one night when you paused mid-story, and very slowly just told people that God loved every last one of them. Forgive me, but you didn't say it with great profundity or eloquence. Just simply, with warmth and feeling, you said, 'God loves you so very much.' The place was very still, and as I looked out at the crowd, some were wiping away tears. It's the basis of everything, isn't it, Adrian? That we are loved. Perhaps we too often assume, wrongly, that everyone knows that, deep down. Perhaps there is so much hurt because our assumption is quite wrong. It's easier to believe that God loves the world, but tough to believe – really, really believe – that he loves me.

Anyway, I so enjoyed the tour.

How are you, Adrian? Yes, I really do want to know.

Much love,

Jeff

THREE

Hello Jeff,

Congratulations on inventing a new word. Wettage. Brilliant!

It's the kindly roving pervert here. So good to hear from you, and especially to be reminded so graphically that I am not the only one who spends his time juggling with confusion and idiocy and a passionate desire to see the love of God making a difference in people's lives. Sometimes, by a ludicrously frantic effort, I manage to keep all three of these awkwardly-shaped objects in the air at the same time. More often than not, though, I drop one, lunge to regain it, and lose my grip on the other two. I'm not joking. It drives me mad.

Speaking of all this, you asked me a question in your letter, something to do with whether I feel raw after each of the acts of buffoonery that punctuate my life with such unremitting frequency. I am going to answer that question, but in a rather roundabout way, beginning with a little story.

Two weeks ago, I was waiting to buy a cup of coffee in a hospital canteen near King's Lynn. At the front of the queue, an elderly husband and wife were paying for their lunch. I don't know if you're familiar with the enchanting

Norfolk accent. It varies a little from place to place in the county, but generally speaking it's characterised by a slow, measured tone, and unusually elongated vowel sounds. This is especially the case at the end of a sentence, where the voice does a little upward tilt, transforming just about every utterance into an interrogative. As the wife chose a piece of fruit to go with her sandwich, she addressed the fellow behind the counter.

'I like pe-e-e-a-rs. He like pe-e-e-a-rs. I like 'em ha-a-a-rd. He like 'em so-o-o-ft. So he never gets any . . .'

This singularly ungenerous lady might have been surprised and puzzled to learn that her words struck a particular chord in me because I had been looking closely at the book of Malachi in connection with a week-long house party Bridget and I recently led at Scargill House.

Familiar with Malachi, Jeff? Last book in the Old Testament. It's more or less one long holy rant from God about the pathetic sacrifices being offered by priests at the altar: manky old goats, flea-ridden pigeons, half-dead sheep, that sort of thing.

'Ask your governor if he'd put up with that,' says God indignantly. 'I'm not pleased with you or your useless fires, and I'm not going to accept any offering from your hands.'

If you want to bring the whole thing up to date, here's a very simple way to express it:

God doesn't like garage flowers.

He's not interested in the hastily assembled fag-ends of our time or energy or money or commitment. Why would he be?

'You weep, and accuse me of not answering your prayers,' he complains, 'but do you answer *my* prayers? If all you have to offer is useless garbage that you've got no use for anyway, then quite frankly I'd rather have nothing.'

'*Rather have nothing.*' How about that?

One of the things I did realise during our week of study was that, despite the uncompromising power of this rant, there is one imperfect sacrifice that God will willingly, happily accept from me, whenever I decide to offer it. What is it? Well, quite simply (and ominously in one sense), it's me; Adrian Plass. Jeff Lucas. Anyone else who's mad or brave enough to follow through the Good Friday, Bad Saturday, Easter Sunday pattern that continually, painfully, benevolently invades our space if we allow it in.

Sorry about the sermonising. It was more for me than for you.

So, what's this got to do with answering your question? I suppose it's something to do with the disturbing place I find myself in at the moment, a place that swirls with issues of vanity, independence, fear of the unknown and advancing age. How would I summarise my problem? Okay, I think I can get it down to four words.

God doesn't need me.

Peter would have understood what I'm talking about. After his courtyard catastrophe he might have said something like this:

Why was I weeping? Him. His fault. Stupid Jesus. He didn't want me. He didn't need me. Do you know, he talked to me sometimes as if I was some dark, terrible person – fiend – trying to drag him away from his blessed, blasted pathway to whatever horrible thing he's convinced has to happen to him.

He actually called me Satan once. Me! Me! He needs to sort his ideas out. I mean, I can't be the rock he's going to build his church on and Satan as well, can I? You tell me. Perhaps I can. Perhaps I'm thick.

The thing is, you're supposed to help your friends, aren't you? And I would have done. I'm not saying I wasn't scared, but when they came for him in the garden, I actually got my sword out, and I honestly think I would have died for him if I had to. Know what I mean? It was worth getting cut to pieces for that man – because I loved him. That's what you do when you love someone, isn't it? You use everything you've got, and you don't think about the consequences, you just get in there and do it.

And what did he say? 'Put your sword away. If I wanted I could ask my father and he'd send twelve legions of angels to get me out of here.' Well, why didn't he? Why not? What was his silly problem? Some kind of wild, lunatic independence? Doesn't need me! Doesn't need my sword! Doesn't need his Father's angels. Doesn't need any damn thing except this – this ghastly, black thing that has to happen for reasons that only he understands. What is he on about? What is he on about? What is he *on* about?

Why did I say I didn't know him? Oh, I don't know. I don't know. I do know. I was embarrassed about people thinking I was tied up with this – loser.

I was hurt. He didn't need me, not *me*, not the me that would have done *anything* for him apart from – well, apart from trailing along behind him into dark, hopeless, pointless misery. Oh, dear God, I wish he hadn't looked at me! His eyes! Oh, I love him, and I'm so sorry. And I would give any-thing – anything to have another chance.

It isn't going to happen. I've blown it. It isn't going to hap-pen . . .

To put it another way, and bearing in mind what hap-pened at Peter's subsequent breakfast encounter with the risen Jesus, now that I know he doesn't need me, I'm beginning to realise just how useful I could be. If I lay this sacrifice down on the altar, the sacrifice of personal responsibility for, and ownership of the effect that my writing and speaking and other bits of ministry might have, what is left for me? You ask me if I feel raw as a result of my buffoonery? Well yes, but not half as raw as I feel when I stand in a pulpit or on a stage and am filled with the certain knowledge that I will always be a rusty old jalopy driven by God with a smile on his face. (Checked your brakes lately, Jeff?)

It happened the other day, actually. I was feeling like one of those scummy pieces of rag that get lost behind a radiator for three months, and I had to climb into a pulpit and preach to three hundred people. Ironically, and I think you'll understand this, feeling like a useless git made it easier in a way. I leaned back and reported on things I'd learned about God. Couldn't go wrong really. But what about me? Where was I? What was I? An item of speaking equipment. A postman. A humble servant? Humble-shumble!

Do you know, Jeff, I think there were times when Jesus came close to feeling something like this weird dislocation. Far worse in his case. He was a man who was also God. How strange is that? How did he deal with it? There's a poem in *Silences and Nonsenses*, my book of collected poetry, which tentatively explores this very question.[1] It's called 'What of Me?' Here it is.

Yes, he will rise again
But what of me?
Though death flaps down to take me like a huge black bird
Casting ragged shadows over lilies of the valley
Over milky moonlit seas

Sunrise glory
Sunset flame
Peach and pearl in Galilean skies
The coolness of a woman's hand
Children's eyes
The rasp of rough-grained wood against the skin
Light in the gaze of men, who, by a miracle of faith,
    have seen
Heard, walked, talked
Discovered that their pitted skin is whole and clean
Sabbath walks, meandering through rolling fields of wheat
The chattering and chuckling of my friends
Their sweet naivety
A scent of cooking fish
The call to eat
Old stories by the fire
Good wine
A kiss
Love and wisdom in my mother's smile
The tears of those who loved me much
Because I gently, fiercely took away their sin
And will I rise again?
Indeed, the Son of Man must rise and live once more
But what of me?
What of me?

Every time, Jeff. Every single time. Every time I think I'm going to lose it and run screaming into some kind of sweet enfolding darkness, I'm rescued by Jesus whispering the same words in my ear.

'Been there. Done that. Got the loincloth.'

He's so annoying, and so lovely.

God bless,
        Adrian

FOUR

Hi Adrian,

I've been pondering your last letter, in which you say, I think with considerable relief, that the one imperfect sacrifice that God will accept is you, us.

And that took me back to your first letter, where you shared the beautiful image of that little boy at Scargill, who placed cushions under the parts of the cross where he thought Jesus would have felt the most pain. There are so many stunning aspects to that scene. I wish I could have been there to see it.

But as I've reflected on that moment, I love that the little boy worshipped without any words. Picking up cushions and tenderly placing them is what he did for Jesus. I'd like to learn how to do that.

Sometimes I don't worship because I feel the pressure to talk; to say something sensible or profound to God. My mumbled syllables of adoration seem pathetic; not so much gold, frankincense and myrrh, more polystyrene, Brut and Old Spice. More club crooner than opera singer. It's not that I fear that God will be displeased by what I mutter to him: just bored by it.

I'm trying to learn to just be with Jesus, without actually saying anything; to just let him look at me, and somehow find a way for me to focus on him. It's hard, though, isn't it? Most of the time I feel like my 'eyes' of faith have terrible cataracts. I'm like Peter, who just had to blurt something out on the Mount of Transfiguration, and put his size thirteen sandal in his mouth. Imagine it – Moses, Elijah and Jesus are right there, in an epic luminous parade, and Peter has this deep need to say something. He was trying to be helpful, but what tumbled out of his mouth was ridiculous, as he proposed putting up sheds for the star players of God's big story. He's got a front row seat for what truly was the greatest show on earth, and he's pondering building a shanty town.

And so God has to quieten him down. A voice from a cloud effectively puts a finger on Peter's lips: 'This is my Son, whom I love. Listen to him!' At last another miracle occurs: Peter stops talking. I'd like to learn how to do the same when I'm worshipping or praying; to just be.

Perhaps that's why I've found a new appreciation for liturgy over the last few years. It all began when a Bishop friend of mine gave me a copy of *Common Worship*. I thanked him for it warmly, but was inwardly wrinkling my nose at the thought of using it. The gift was initially as attractive as a packet of pork scratchings to a rabbi. But when I opened the book, and began to read, my attitude changed, even though I was confused by the whole thing.

It was the church calendar that befuddled me. I am a non-conformist (I hate that term, it makes me sound like I'm with the crowd who like to argue with everything. Come to think of it . . .). We non-Anglicans know our Christmas and Easter, mainly because of the sudden seasonal flurry of trees and eggs, but we are prone to getting our Epiphanies mixed up with our Septuagesimas.

And there were other challenges with using a prayer book. I didn't know what to do with the bits that were crafted for congregational response: 'The Lord be with you.' 'And also with you.' So I did both bits, but with different voices, which must have seemed strange to any passersby. Hearing two voices coming out of the same lips could be a red flag to anyone with a penchant for exorcism, tempting them to grab a garland of garlic and cast something out of me. But I grew to love the words in that book, because I didn't have to create them. I could just make them my own.

I recently spent four days with an Anglo-Catholic group. I loved the scattering of the holy water, and the wafting of incense (although it made me cough: it's hard to cough reverently). The priests in their gorgeous vestments, the flickering of tall candles, the beautifully dressed altar – all of this stirred my evangelical soul, and I enjoyed the theatre of it all. But the best part of it was the liturgy. There were moments when I felt that through the liturgy, the congregation picked me up and carried me.

Let me explain. Kay and I are proud grandparents to the gorgeous Stanley, who is three. He, together with his younger brother, Alex, are two of the greatest sources of delight in our lives. When we take Stanley out shopping, his favourite thing is to walk between us and hold our hands; he loves us to swing him along the high street rather than walk. He squeals and giggles as we carry him down the road.

In sharing liturgy, I was picked up and carried along by the words spoken by others. Sometimes I didn't say them at all, but just nodded as everyone else did, and occasionally just muttered: 'Yep, Jesus, ditto from me. What they're saying – take that from me too.' I can see how liturgy could be so sustaining when life is difficult or tragic, and we trudge through days that are so horrid, they render us speechless. The experience was so empowering, and I lived with a new sense of peace for ages. Scratch that: I still feel sustained to this day. So I was moved by the image of that child, silently placing those cushions under the cross.

Of course, the really glorious thing is that when that happened, Jesus noticed and smiled. Our worship, however we present it, seems so tiny, doesn't it? Yet it is received, even welcomed. And yes, that includes the imperfect sacrifices of ourselves.

I often feel a little like another small boy probably felt; you know, the one who only had his lunch to offer to Jesus when there were five thousand mouths to be fed. But then, that little incident turned out well, didn't it?

With love,

Jeff

FIVE

Hello Jeff,

Thanks for your last letter, and thanks also for speaking with such honesty about the problem of words and worship, how they come together, and how we maintain authenticity in the process. While we're on that subject by the way, you may recall that when we were touring last year, the evening usually ended with me reading an exceptionally silly poem called 'In a Parallel Universe', written as an ice-breaker for a week here at Scargill when we tackled the whole subject of authenticity in Christian living. In case you've forgotten, here it is:

In a parallel universe
The DFS sale really does end
Cliff Richard actually *is* a living doll
A stitch in time holds the morning together
A good-natured Englishman wins the singles trophy
    at Wimbledon

In a parallel universe
The Archbishop of Canterbury is a short, bald woman
Garages are not allowed to sell flowers
Stainless steel teapots pour perfectly

There is only one category of rubbish, collected weekly
    by nice, rather poetic people

In a parallel universe
Airlines pay *us* to fly with them
The sun shines at night when it's needed, not during the
    day when it's light anyway
Each year at least one GCSE English student who is studying
    Wuthering Heights actually reads *Wuthering Heights*
Teenagers don't have to be lent money by their parents in
    order to repay their parents the money they owe them

In a parallel universe
Weather forecasts provide information, in advance,
    about the weather
My wife will be wrong – sometimes
Artificial sweeteners *do* taste like sugar
Children don't leave school believing that Paul Gauguin
    played football for Spurs

In a parallel universe
The sound of a fire alarm going off indicates that there
    might be a fire
Chickens can cross the road without needing to have
    their motivation questioned
IKEA products look as good when you get them home
    as they did in the store
And most importantly of all, fat, and cream, and chocolate,
    and cake and red wine are your five-a-day requirements
    for healthy living

All very silly, but there is a need for the church to seriously consider the question of authenticity, especially in
worship. My own experience has been similar to yours in

some ways. When I was climbing out of my interminably discussed stress illness more than two decades ago, the only kind of church where I could feel comfortable was one where the formality of the occasion and the fixed patterns of liturgy held my troubled, wobbling soul in place until the service came to an end. Sit, stand, respond, sing, kneel, confess, stand again, kneel again, pray, listen, sing again, shake hands with the vicar at the door and go home. It suited me. Ironically, I was able to make a more genuinely individual response to God from the safety and comfort of democratically uniform behaviour, than if I had been crouching miserably in some converted aircraft hangar watching desperate husbands and wives wrestle for possession of the baby in order to avoid the twin horrors of individual freedom and looming ministry.

A positive spin-off from this part of my life was the increased enjoyment of liturgical prayer. As I may have said to you in one of my previous letters, Jeff, I find true beauty in the Prayer of Humble Access that precedes an Anglican communion.

> We do not presume to come to this thy table, O merciful Lord, trusting in our own righteousness, but in thy manifold and great mercies. We are not worthy so much as to gather up the crumbs under thy table. But thou art the same Lord, whose property is always to have mercy . . .

Bejewelled prose and I love it, but here's a weird thing. Nowadays I tend to be happiest with the two extremes, this kind of beautifully written heartfelt prose, or a kind of wordless, bemused anticipation of God's indefinable, strangely ordinary presence. In between these poles there are forms of Christianity that terrify me. The worst ones are cobbled together out of pulpy words and pale optimism and an overwhelming desire to huddle inside boundaries that are so low you could trip over them if you ever dared go near enough to find out.

Formal or informal: that's how you might label the modes that appeal to me, but there are dangers here as well, and I've been pushed into thinking a lot about this recently.

There's been a lot of talk at the Christian centre where I work about marketing. How do you sell a product whose heart is (or is supposed to be) the ministry of the Holy Spirit to those who are in need? There are no easy answers to this question, bearing in mind the eternal balance between financial viability and spiritual authenticity, but one comment struck me particularly. It was suggested that, for the sake of fundraising and the building of our status in the wider Christian community, the public face of the centre should wear a more formal and confident expression of what we are and what we can offer:

We are an ecumenical and intentional community in the tradition of New Monasticism . . .

Meanwhile, through such avenues as blogs, the 'informal' face of Scargill would be revealed. When I first heard about this, I shrugged and nodded and grunted assent like you do, but later a sort of light seemed to dawn. Hold on a moment, I thought, our informal face is what we actually are. The long nights, wrestling with resentment and puzzlement over the behaviour of other community members, or with nagging guilt about our own. The moments of sheer wonder when God moves into a cold, dark space, bringing a miracle of warmth and light into someone's life. The gritty, gutty requirement to be truly honest and cliché-free when listening to a tear-filled account of three miscarriages, one still-birth and the subsequent discovery of liver cancer, from a woman who has prayed and prayed and prayed until all she has left is the choice of abandoning faith or trusting the God who has disappointed, whatever he does or doesn't do for her in the future. The laughter and conviviality that rings through the place often and effectively enough for us to be sure that friendship and humour are prayers and answers to prayers in themselves. The times when all you want is to be somewhere else altogether.

It's a holy mess, Jeff, this face of ours. More interesting than beautiful. And it reminds me of the ministry of Jesus, a ministry that he steadfastly protected from artificial formality, however hard other people tried to push him into kingship or false consistency or the manipulative use of miraculous power. His heart became heavy, he wept, he came near to being crushed by grief, he was disappointed and he was shocked. These things were as real and as much a part of his life as the healings and the good times with his friends and the congratulations of his Father.

That is the expression on his face, and it is how people will view us if we ever get round to truly reflecting his life. Jesus was really poor at marketing, and he changed the world.

Fancy a beer, Jeff?

Lots of love,

Adrian

SIX

Dear Adrian,

Yes, sharing a beer (or better still, one each) would be great.

Having read your last letter three times (it brought a strange sense of relief to me), I've been thinking a little more about why it is that I'm developing such a liking for liturgy. I think it's this: the words of the creeds are solid and trustworthy, without being clichéd. Of course, they are only words, so they are limited. Trying to describe God is a little like lobbing snowballs up at the moon, don't you think, Adrian? The best we can do is get the snowballs about twenty feet up on their journey, which is paltry considering the moon is around a quarter of a million miles away from us. At least the words of the creeds are a good start.

There are far too many wobbly words in the world – and in the Christian world at that. You mentioned earlier that God doesn't like those nasty pallid looking flowers that garages sell: I have a theory that he doesn't appreciate plastic garden furniture either. You know the type I mean, Adrian? You park yourself in one of those white plastic chairs, only to discover that they're perilously flimsy, and your pleasant moment with a Pimms and lemonade is ruined because you're unexpectedly flat on your back on the patio.

Technology (and particularly social networking) means that there are millions of words in circulation, and some of the clichés that regularly do the rounds amongst Christians nudge me to despair. It happened again only today. On Facebook, this morning, someone posted that 'Faith is not believing that God can do something, it's believing that He will do something!!!' The three exclamation marks showed the breathless excitement with which this statement was made, all of which leaves *me* breathless. It only takes a momentary engagement of a brain cell to realise that it is complete tosh. Unless God has emphatically informed us of his precise future plans (and that usually involves him despatching an angel with a newsflash, which is rare), most of the time we simply just don't know what he is going to do, and saying otherwise means we're engaging in empty presumption. God has this habit of being God, and although I might bluster that I know the outcome of that cancer treatment or this family crisis, I don't. 'Faith' of the sort that bosses God around, or tries to make him a divine genie in a bottle, is deeply unreliable, and destined to go the way of the plastic garden chair that succumbed when my huge Auntie Gladys tried to insert her considerable bottom into it. But there's something reassuringly musty and solid as oak about the creeds. They've stood the test of a lot of time, and millions have rested their weight on them, and they have held firm.

You mentioned marketing. I too have been wondering about how we 'market' Christianity. I'm terribly worried about the much-marketed promise that those who follow Jesus will be strong as a result. Sometimes I see advertisements for conferences that make me want to run away and hide: 'Come and take your place in the Global Convocation of God's Winning Warriors!' Eh? Who would have the barefaced audacity to show up for such an event? Is there a seminar stream entitled 'Humility for those who consider themselves to be winning warriors' in the programme? Do I have to be nominated as a winner, or just designate myself as one?

I find it all exhausting, Adrian. Perhaps we should start our own event: 'Come and take your place in the parochial huddle of prats . . . all welcome, except those who think they've graduated from prattishness . . .'

Jesus was not always strong. He was unable to control his emotions at times. He found Gethsemane to be a lonely place, and pleaded with his friends to watch with him, pray with him, just be with him and stay awake. And his last words before death were an anguished cry of abandonment. It's hardly a portrait of the traditional warrior.

With that in mind, I have decided that I'd like to be like a little yellow bird that's been hanging around at our house in Colorado. For the last few weeks, we have been summoned muttering from sleep by its dawn chorus of praise. Sleep deprivation is not the only result of our verbose yellow visitor: our back deck is encrusted by poo meringues. Someone told me that if I bought a large plastic owl from the plastic garden furniture shop, this would frighten our bird friend away. Wrong. The imitation owl has now become a comfortable perch for our meringue-producing feathered friend.

My theory is that the bird is endlessly looking for his parents. A few months ago I discovered a nest on our back deck, and on closer inspection, discovered that it contained a gaggle of fluffy, scrawny little yellow blobs whose sole gifting in life seemed to be squawking at their mother for food. Now the nest family has scattered, but this particular adolescent won't give up his family that easily. He desperately wants to be with them again.

I think I'd like to be neither strong nor weak, but just endlessly wanting to be where Jesus is, taking part in what he is doing.

One more thing while we're on the subject of marketing. You mentioned Scargill. I've been thinking about the way organisations and companies present themselves. Most groups have mission statements and slogans which (they hope) sum up what they do and who they are. Once you describe yourself in a certain way, however, there's the perilous possibility that you might think that because you *call* yourself that, then that's what you *are*.

I was musing on this during a recent transatlantic flight that took seventy hours (okay, it was nine, it just felt like seventy). The airline concerned touts itself as 'The Friendly Skies', which was so 100 per cent wrong that it was almost laughable.

Parked in coach class, we were treated with the wrinkled-nose disdain that one usually reserves for people who make big bad smells in small lifts. Any request (like for water, hardly a luxury in the dehydrating atmosphere of an aircraft) was greeted as an intrusion. The flight attendants seemed more intent on having a staff reunion than looking after their passengers, and treated us all like naughty children who mess up the Sunday School outing by inserting a squirming crab down the back of old Miss Hitchens' knickers. At the end of the flight, the purser made an announcement which implied that we were long lost relatives with whom she was sharing a tearful goodbye, and we wondered why she had treated us like we were an embarrassing rash for which no cream was available. I've seen this in churches – those that bang on endlessly about how important relationships are, often have very poor relationships . . .

Once we make statements about ourselves, we find ourselves under pressure to live up to them. The church that announces 'Come to our exciting worship service expecting a miracle' has just given itself two huge problems. If we (a) tell people to come expecting a miracle, then some will come expecting a miracle. Splendid if one happens . . . and (b) no church can be exciting all the time, every week. I've been to some of these places, where everything is described as awesome, including the preaching, the building, and the coffee that's served afterwards. A Hawaiian sunset is awesome, the Great Barrier Reef is awesome. A crushed coffee bean in water, however, is pleasant – but not awesome.

I call this kind of church 'orgasmochurch'. I'm not being wantonly crude; I think the analogy is a useful one. If everything is centred around an epic spine-chilling head-turning heart-warming Holy Ghost explosion experience, then every service has to be more exhilarating than the last. If it's not, then those looking for 'the next big move of God' will transfer to the more exciting church down the road as they continue their experiential safari. So what to do when you're a leader and you've marketed the church you lead as exciting and miracle-laden? You fake it. You may not consciously fake it, and you didn't set out to create a sham. But you do.

Enough of my ranting, Adrian. You asked if I'd like a beer? Certainly. We have a lovely pub on the corner. Real ale. Friendly staff. And no plastic garden chairs.

SEVEN

Dear Jeff,

Here I am again, settling into our two-man 'parochial huddle of prats'. Quite a comfortable place to be actually, and a useful arena in which to get some depressingly dirty water off my chest. There's always something, isn't there? Always some shift of emphasis or swing of the pendulum that takes us Christians into a place that sits messily, like one of your bird blobs on the continuum between unhelpful and downright bad. I think it was your mention of Christian clichés that triggered a particular memory. I was involved in a conference a few years ago where the youth work was being led by a group of young adults who certainly didn't lack enthusiasm and goodwill, but had clearly spent far too much time studying *The Observer's Book of Christian Sound-bites*. I'm sure you are toe-curlingly familiar with this collection of cheap sweets wrapped in shiny paper. Examples?

'If God's not beside you any more – guess who moved.'

'It may be in your head, but has it dropped the eighteen inches to your heart?'

And it really is not just about these banal sets of words. Rather, it is about a mind-set that will not (or dare not)

allow raggedness, humanity, individual differences or
varieties of spiritual journeying to be part of what it means
to find Jesus. I am all too aware that some folk will inter-
pret the last item on this list as a suggestion that I am
embracing the idea that all religions, Christianity included,
are different lights shed through facets of the same crystal.
I certainly am not, Jeff. Jesus is the way, the truth and the
life, but even a cursory reading of the New Testament
shows that the Master will graciously and ingeniously
meet people at unexpected and surprising points in *their*
journey, not his.

It is as though some group of Scotland-worshipping
fanatics were to insist that the only possible way to reach
Edinburgh from London is via Leicester and the A74, in a
reconditioned Hillman Imp. Not true. Not sensible. Not
the way things are. Not quite sane.

Anyway, this group of young people that I mentioned
just now did their good-natured but rather simplistic
thing all week, and were probably quite unaware that at
least two of the people in their group had been repelled
and disappointed by the way in which faith had been presented. One young man spoke to me about the meaning-
ful and circuitous route he had taken thus far towards the
possibility of faith, and described his disappointment on
hearing Christianity expressed in such 'narrow' terms. He
needed to be opened up, not closed down. Unfortunately,
there is a subtle form of mob rule that can occur in groups
of believers who are not quite as sure of their ground as
they would like to be. Unlike most mobs, however, these
uneasy cohorts tend not to attack, but to retreat into garrisons designed to withstand the challenges of truth and
reality. Only one small door is available for those of us
who might consider entering, and we do have to get the
password exactly right.

Am I exaggerating? Well, I do get a bit worried when I find myself ranting on like this, but then I think of something that happened just the other day. I was sitting outside a marquee at one of our major Christian events pretending to read a book, and listening as a group of delightful young people at the next table chattered excitedly about the ways in which God was working in their lives. Sweet and frightening it was, Jeff. I can recall one or two scraps of the conversation.

'Jessica's really prophetic, but I don't think she's quite as prophetic as Sam, and Rachel's just amazing! She's like, 'God says this about you . . .', and it's wow! You know, it's just so incredible!'

'This fantastic speaker said the Holy Spirit was going to come in power, and just after he said that, people were, you know, being healed all over the place. God was so there! Know what I mean? It was awesome!'

Charming really, and the idea of trying to squash those high spirits is too horrible for words, but the whole thing scared me silly, for them, for those they encounter, for the church of the future and for God, who, in my not very humble opinion, simply does not distribute these things like confetti at a wedding. The culture of vivid, spiritual immediacy is a very attractive one, especially to young people, but it has to be genuine, doesn't it? It seems to me that emphasis on words rather than substance is an all too familiar recipe for disappointment.

What do you think, Jeff? Am I just a grumpy old Christian who can't leave people alone to enjoy their harmless fun, or is there actually a battle to be fought in these areas? Whatever the ultimate answer to that question might be, I shall probably go on fighting my corner and hoping that it happens to be God's corner as well. I can't help it. Just to prove that, here's another rant, if you can bear to read it.

Have you noticed how we Christians have finally settled on a comfortably neutral way to talk about the suggestion that God has spoken to us? Previously the options were as follows:

'The word of the Lord came to me, saying . . .' Don't think so.

'God said something interesting while we chatted over coffee this morning . . .' No, he didn't.

'God has given me a word for you . . .' Never during Scrabble for some reason.

'God told me . . .' Too cocksure by half, and impossible to argue with.

The last of these is the one that our new compromise seeks and manages to avoid. The aim is to establish a finely balanced point somewhere between repellent certainty and unconvincing vagueness. Here it is:

'I felt the Lord saying . . .'

What do you think, Jeff? Have we cracked it? Does the gently implied humility of *feeling* rather than *hearing* make our claim to have received a communication from God more or less acceptable or convincing? Or have we lost our grip and our nerve when it comes to the highly desirable gift of prophecy? I don't know what you think, but I feel the Lord is saying . . .

The serious side of all this is that we believers, yearning quite reasonably for a little stability and predictability in our Christian experience, will put up with all sorts of pale, misleading and even actively destructive attacks on the advance of the kingdom of God, as long as those attacks reinforce the religious status quo that garrisons us against unwelcome interference by God in our lives. In this context, one of my current rants concerns the essential and incomprehensible fact that Jesus was truly man as well as being truly God. I might say a little more about that in another letter, but in the meantime here's a piece that got me into trouble recently with a few people. Perhaps it pushes the point a little too much in the other direction, but not-too-far is nowhere sometimes. This very silly monologue is spoken to God by the angel detailed to ensure that a dove lands on Jesus' head just before he is baptised. Well, we all make mistakes, even angels – well, especially angels sometimes . . .

Dove, not Duck

Yes, Lord, good morning, I am reporting to you as the angel responsible for the debacle that occurred yesterday. Yes, of course I am extremely sorry and deeply embarrassed about the mistake that was indeed made by er – me. Sorry? Yes, I know. I know now that you said 'dove', I know that now. You said 'dove', but I heard 'duck'. I heard 'duck'. And so I procureth an duck, with considerable difficulty I might add, and I placed it on your Son's head as instructed. Well, yes, quite – as I believed I had been instructed. Because I did not hear 'dove', I heard 'duck'. No, I am not calling your omnipotence into question, Lord. But I heard 'duck'. Who made the ears? Who made the ears? Sorry! Sorry, Lord!

What? Yes, it was an exceeding fat bird, and I would have to agree, it did overhang thy Son's face so that only his nose and mouth could be seen. Yes, several bystanders did enquire why he appeareth inexplicably to be wearing a duck mask. And yes the extraordinarily loud quacking was unfortunate, interrupting, as you rightly point out, your very moving words of affirmation from above, and detracting somewhat from the dignity of thy speech.

The thing is, Lord, I know you said dove, but I thought you said – Sorry? Yes, it was a difficult moment when the bird fell off his head halfway through. Well, in mine own defence, doves would have been ten a penny (if I'd heard 'dove', I heard 'duck'), and the only trained duck I could get at short notice was a very old, grossly overweight mallard called Boris, and Boris does not like heights. What? No, Lord, not even six feet off the ground. Doesn't do flying any more. He said that. 'I don't do flying.' He gets very giddy. He just lost his balance, Lord. His eyes started rolling, and he fell off. What you need to understand, Lord, is that whereas you probably did say 'dove', I actually heard – '

Ow! That empty can of Ambrosia really hurt my head, Lord. Well, you may have shouted 'Duck!', but I heard 'Dove . . .'

Looking forward to hearing from you, Jeff.
        Love, Adrian

EIGHT

Dear Adrian,

Lovely to hear from you. I find these 'prat-to-prat' exchanges hugely refreshing, because our correspondence assures me that either I am normal and there are lots of other limping followers of Jesus around (like you) who are not exactly marching to Zion (as the hymn suggests) but staggering along with the ungainly gait normally associated with those who have had one too many. Of course the other alternative is that we are both quite mad and should try to get a group rate for therapy.

I'm aware that all this honest talk could get us both into hot water. Sometimes Christians don't speak up about their darkest fears because they're afraid of how they'll be perceived. Awkward questions are stifled because we're nervous that a heresy hunter will leap from the shadows and slap a 'liberal' label on our foreheads.

It's ironic that we're not more at home with truth. A leading figure in American Christian publishing recently told me that I am 'too honest for the Christian market' which seems a bit odd, considering we claim to be followers of the Jesus who called himself the truth with a capital 'T'. But despite the possibility of some scolding, surely it's worth pursuing the truth at all or any cost. Truth sets us free. Untruth locks us up.

So to answer your question, I don't think that you are *just* being a grumpy old Christian (though I'm sure you have a capacity for having grumpy days, or perhaps even decades) and you and I both *are* becoming increasingly old (someone offered me an over-sixties discount yesterday, and I'm only fifty-six. Hmmmph). These questions must be raised, otherwise people will be imprisoned by a faith that isn't true and therefore doesn't work. And when they find out, they might be tempted to chuck the faith towel in altogether. How tragic it is when Christians are oppressed by the slogans of other believers, some of whom were apparently previously self-employed as advisors to Job.

I saw a vivid example of this at yet another Christian conference that I spoke at last week. Do you ever feel like an emotional and spiritual refugee at these events, Adrian? I really enjoy the sense of belonging, but there are times when I feel estranged from the Christianity presented at these large bashes. To be clear, I believe in the value of big celebrations, and not just because they keep the likes of me and you in work. It seems to me that God has always provided his people with feasts and festivals, parties with a purpose to remind us of who we are. Circumcision prior to the invention of anaesthetic was also part of the programme to prevent an identity crisis, which I wouldn't be quite so keen on. Anyway, back to that refugee feeling . . .

One speaker suggested that the devil will be driven away simply by yelling at him. Wow. Now we know how the problem of evil in the Universe can be resolved: just get the people of God a loud hailer apiece, or, better still, built-in amplification. That'll send the powers of darkness packing.

The impression was given that being a Christian meant life is endlessly epic, and our Tuesday mornings should be loaded with angelic encounters and all kinds of other sparkly happenings. I bristled at this, because although I've had more than my fair share of 'God moments', that doesn't change the fact that much of life – including the Christian life – is uneventful.

Anyway, when it was my turn to preach, I made some statements about what real faith looks like, which, if I read the Bible correctly, is mostly about endurance. I am so wearied by the endless clichés ('Christian sound-bites', I think you called them) that emerge whenever cancer rears its ugly head or it looks like someone is about to die. Some move into bullish denial, insisting that the wretched disease will have to retreat because we've prayed that it will. Others suggest that there must be something terribly wrong with the sufferer – that they have unwittingly provided a landing strip for the dark hawk of disease to alight upon. Perhaps the cancer sufferer's grandfather was a Freemason. Excellent news. Now they have to pay a subscription to a genealogy website and perform some odd ceremony to disconnect from their apron-wearing ancestor, or perhaps even dig them up and slap them.

Or maybe the patient is nursing some hidden sin, or doesn't have enough faith. Wonderful. Not only is the sufferer wrestling with excruciating pain: now they think God is angry with them as well. In the wake of this madness, two tragedies are added to the terminal illness. First, people don't get to say goodbye. An admission that death is near is tantamount to failure and a lack of faith. So little preparation is made and words of love and appreciation go unsaid. Worse, sometimes Christians die smothered by a suffocating sense of shame. A friend told me

that his lovely, faithful father had been hesitant to admit
that it looked like he was going to expire, 'because he
didn't want to let the prayer team down.' He lived an A+
life of faith and love, but died with a sense of 'B minus –
could do better' on his spiritual report card.

Anyway, I shared my angst about all this during my
sermon – and got rather excited about it, to the point that
I think I shouted a little while I was preaching – which I
regret. I don't like preachers who yell, especially me. But
I was animated and angry.

The next morning I wandered into the large venue
where people were gathering, and started chatting to a
smiling, silver-haired lady who was parked in a wheelchair. She hadn't been to a church service for a year,
because every time she rolls herself in, some keen
Christian either tells her exactly why she is wheelchair
bound, or insists that she get out the chair and walk, pron-
to. After a while, this nudged her into a deep depression,
so she stayed away. The night before I had apologised to
people with disabilities, fearing that many of them had
been experimented on by breathless, well-meaning
people, who had bruised them with their slogans.
Apparently, Adrian, that lovely lady felt an incredible
sense of relief, as though a weight had been lifted from
her. She spent a couple of hours talking late into the night
with her son, and when she met some of her friends that
morning, they made the strangest comment to her.
Apparently her skin had turned grey over the year:
depression had relentlessly sucked all rose from her
cheeks. But now they noted that her skin had changed
colour: the grey had been banished.

And that got me thinking. Is it possible that unreality
and hyper-faith have actually robbed people of life and
energy, and turned them into black and white imitations

of what should be their full-on Technicolor selves? That's why I think that our grumpy questions are vital. Grey is not a good colour for the skin, or the soul.

Before I go, there's a phrase that you used in your last letter that I wanted to pick up on. You talked about 'mob rule' – that when some Christians get together and share their spiritual experiences, something ugly can happen. Anyone who asks questions about those experiences is made to feel insufficiently spiritual and out of step. I've been around some of this. Someone stands up on Sunday morning and insists that God has given them a bizarre and utterly incomprehensible picture – you know, they see a Japanese Samurai warrior wrestling with a Croatian midget, and winning the fight by dumping them into a vat of cold custard – that sort of thing. Everyone who hears it seriously wonders about the validity of the picture and considers sidling up to the picture-sharer and proffering the number of the NHS helpline . . .

. . . but they don't. Afraid of being rejected for not 'getting it', we mumble and nod and agree and just go along with the madness. A creeping Gnosticism drives this mob rule, where some insist that they are deeper than others, and any criticism or evaluation of their behaviour means that the questioner is just not sufficiently in love with Jesus to understand. Honest conversation becomes impossible. But I'd rather risk the ire of the mob than go along with the madness.

> With love,
> Jeff

PS: I loved the duck. And I'd love you to rant a little more about Jesus becoming fully man. I know of a speaker who got into serious trouble for suggesting that Jesus would have needed to do very human things, like go to the toilet. Wow. What do we think he did for 33 years?

PPS: I talked about 'large gatherings'. I was in a church one Sunday morning, and the Pastor stood up and announced that many of the ladies of the church were at a 'Big Women's Conference' which I presume was not sponsored by Weight Watchers. He went on to add that the airline they'd travelled on had mislaid their luggage, and that we should 'pray that the bags get home safely'. Amen to that. And I hope that we both get home safely, too.

NINE

Dear Jeff,

Thanks for your last letter. There are two things I want to say straightaway. First, while I share your despair over incomprehensible pictures from a god who appears to have got all his creative ideas from Salvador Dali, I believe that the custard component (hot rather than cold, naturally) is very much of the Lord. Custard with everything, I say. Family members eating in restaurants with me are continually embarrassed when the time comes to select a dessert course, and I mumble brainlessly to the waiter, 'Is there anything that comes with custard?'

For the same reason, if I was ever offered a choice of prophecies, I would probably say, 'Anything that's available is fine. Japanese warriors, East European dwarfs, pre-war Bakelite suppositories, any image you've got lying around that hasn't been used for a while, fine – as long as it comes with custard.'

That's got that sorted out. Now, the second thing I want to communicate is going to shock you, Jeff. Be ready. Brace yourself. This is it. I am going to say something optimistic.

Now, please don't judge me too harshly. We all have these dips from time to time, and I am no exception. One moment I was trudging miserably along, muttering and moaning my way through life with absolute consistency, when it suddenly dawned on me that I was experiencing something dangerously close to hope. Devastated, I cried out for help and comfort. Nothing! Where is God when you need him?

What am I talking about? I'll try to explain. You spoke in your letter about all sorts of things that are problematic, not just for Christian speakers, but for many, many yearning believers. I can identify with all of them. You described that sense of being alienated at events that are supposed to be inclusively spiritual or, at the very least, Christian. You quoted somebody who said that you were too honest for the Christian market. Picking up a point that I had made, you wrote about the dangers of mob rule in the church, and the difficulty of penetrating a sub-culture that is too fundamentally weak to allow challenge. Then there was the story of the lady in the wheelchair who drew new confidence and comfort from someone speaking out the heart of God in a loud voice in front of lots of people. As a result of this experience her skin lost its grey pallor, and as you rightly say, grey is not a good colour for the skin or the soul.

Has it occurred to you, Jeff, that all of these things precisely reflect the ministry of Jesus (definitely too honest for the Christian market) while he was walking this earth? Read that last paragraph through once more and I think you will understand what I am saying. On a personal level, my friend, I have quite often seen the shadow of self-doubt in you. I know you are not slow to confess that this is the case, but I would like you to feel the same flowering of hope that is beginning to bring delight and confusion into my life. If we truly want to be Jesus for people, then the things you mentioned are the right and proper problems that we are bound to encounter. My way or the highway, says Jesus, and his way almost invariably hurts the feet. That can make you cry when you are on your own, or laugh when you are hobbling along beside someone else. Rejoice and take the pain-killers. You are a gift of God to the church. Hold your nerve.

The tiny flower of hope in me is connected with all this, and it is rooted in an idea that you and I have written and spoken about before. Something to do with giving up. Something to do with actually grasping and putting into practice the notion that removing ourselves from the ingenious activities of God in the lives of those he loves, is ultimately more productive than all the bling, the mantras, the funny voices, the devilish caution, the itch to fix, the fear of failure, the fencing in and out of human feelings and experiences, the patterns, the pomp and the pratting about.

Does this mean that we are not involved? On the contrary. In prayer for guests here at Scargill, for instance, Bridget and I are well aware that we have to be there, listening intently to what is said to us, but minding our own business as far as the spiritually practical response of the Holy Spirit is concerned. Somewhere in the middle of that entrancing tension we glimpse shining possibilities, and later hear of deeply encouraging developments. I certainly don't mean to imply that we are not permitted to use common sense. There have been a couple of encounters recently where a fairly tough approach has been needed just to move people onto square one. A couple we saw recently spent ten minutes telling us how much they loathed their new vicar, and how good it would be for the church if he could be prayed into some sort of ecclesiastical oblivion. Noting the little pool of vitriol gathering around their feet, we pointed out that if they really cared about their church, they would deal with their own attitudes before asking God to dump the devil incarnate who had moved onto their patch. They took it surprisingly well. Rather shocked. I guess it's possible to get so deeply embedded in a view or a prejudice that it becomes invisible.

I suppose the general point I'm trying to make is that God is seriously, seriously less religious than we are. I believe Bonhoeffer talked about aiming for 'religionless Christianity'. I know full well that lots of believers pay lip service to this view, but it is all too easy to slip back into the comfortable corral of churchmanship that makes us feel safe. I'm sure God has no problem at all with his followers enjoying regular sojourns into their own flavour or variety of religious expression but, in the main, those are not the places where the proverbial rubber hits the road – not the one less taken anyway.

All of this is making my faith seem more puzzling, less predictable, considerably more intriguing, and hopeful to the point of something that is beginning to feel suspiciously like satisfaction.

By the way, Jeff, just to fill you in on our present situation, Bridget and I are on Community here at Scargill for at least another year. After that – who knows? Our plan at present is to keep our heads down and hope that God doesn't notice we've gone. I doubt we'll get away with it, though, and it will be interesting to see if another job/episode/involvement has been planned for us. Our move to Yorkshire was the clearest, most unequivocal leading we have experienced, perhaps the only major one.

So, here's a question for you, Jeff. Does God guide people? How does he do it? Why are so many folk struggling with this issue? We meet them all the time. Some

hang on by bleeding fingertips to weak coincidences.
Others poke around among their limited stock of
Christian constructs and precepts, hunting for something
that might make them feel better. What do you think? I'd
like to know, but don't answer the question unless you
feel sure that God is leading you appropriately. Why
don't you lay a fleece or open a door or – er, well, that's
about it really.

      Lots of love,
         Adrian

TEN

Hey Adrian,

Great to hear from you. I am delighted to hear that you are feeling hopeful, and I mean that. I have many faults and weaknesses, including the self-doubt that you astutely mention. Self-doubt regularly attacks me. But being green with envy of other people's nice cars, money, holidays or – even more valuable – their sense of hope – is not one of them. Hope on, I say.

At the end of your letter you mentioned the question of guidance and suggested that I consider discussing this issue, but only after laying a 'fleece'. This 'fleece' term was confusing to me as a new Christian. You and I both know that the phrase originates with the actions of a bewildered chap called Gideon. The idea is that we tell God that if circumstance A happens then we will take that to mean that he is telling us to take action B, and if circumstance C happens, this means that God is asking us to take action D.

In Gideon's case, this involved spreading a woollen fleece on the ground and waiting to see how the early morning dew settled on it – hence the term, 'laying a fleece'. But I didn't understand the context or meaning of all of this when I became a Christian three hundred years ago, and so 'laying a fleece' sounded painful, like laying an egg or passing a kidney stone.

The aforementioned fleece can be anything really – if the next traffic light is green, if my mother-in-law smiles at me, or one can go for the advanced fleece that involves more obscure, unlikely happenings, like being greeted in Sainsbury's by a Japanese sumo wrestler playing the bassoon while standing with one foot immersed in a bucket of custard (sorry to distract you with the mention of custard, Adrian. I know from your last letter that you have an advanced culinary fetish for the yellow stuff. But even you wouldn't want to eat custard tainted by a foot, would you?).

I think that all this fleece-laying is a bit daft, and using Gideon's fleece-laying as justification for it is a bit like using Abraham's knife-wielding over his son Isaac as an example in a parenting seminar. Once again we see that the Bible can be used to fuel some dodgy ideas. Eighteenth-century Christians pointed woodenly to their Bibles to defend slavery and dub the diminutive William Wilberforce as a heretic; the Dutch Reformed Church in South Africa built the vile 'doctrine' of apartheid on a twisted interpretation of the ninth chapter of Genesis.

I digress. Do I believe that God has plans and purposes for our lives? Yes, I do. I think that there are times when he will specifically direct us, like asking you and Bridget to go to Scargill for a season (by the way, I admire you for that. It would take a whole herd of warbling angels to convince me to live in a Christian community, mainly because of the temptations that such an existence would bring, like the strong desire to commit murder).

I do believe that God guides, but I think we can over-egg the idea, and give the impression that we are all getting turn by turn, moment by moment instructions, when we're not. And there's a danger that we try to use God as a GPS system. That's why I'm fond of telling people to stop looking for the will of God. Instead we should look for God himself, and then we'll walk in his broad purposes. All of this matters to me greatly, because in my early years as a Christian, I nearly had a nervous breakdown over the issue of guidance. I was racked with fear that I might miss God's best, which might result in (a) being consigned to uselessness for the rest of my life or (b) God pressing the smite button, which I feared he seemed keen to do. I bought every book I could find about knowing the will of God, having of course prayed that I would buy the book about the will of God that it was the will of God for me to buy . . .

. . . yes. It was all very complicated and confusing.

Someone told me that if I wanted to hear God speak about a specific situation, I should just open my Bible and plunge my finger onto a random verse, which treats Scripture like a lucky dip. As you can imagine, this created utter chaos for me, in all aspects of my life.

Then someone else said God would speak to me if I really want to hear. But how would I know if I *really* wanted to know? The truth is, we often hear what we want to hear. As a preacher, I'm often credited for saying things that have never passed my lips.

I'm sure this happens to you when you speak somewhere, Adrian. As a preacher, it's a frequent occurrence. A bizarre conversation unfolds after the Sunday sermon. A smiling couple approach me, their eyes shining with the look that is often found on the faces of those who believe they have just heard from God:

'Hi Jeff, we wanted to especially thank you for your reference to Latvian clog-dancing during your sermon on the

prodigal son this morning. My wife and I have been thinking and praying about going to Latvia as missionaries and
we're convinced that this is a confirmation that our decision
is correct. And it's amazing that you should mention this on
the very day that we are concluding a forty day fast. Our
lives will never be the same . . .'

I try to gently protest, without shattering their hopes or
rendering their six weeks' abstinence from anything tasty
a waste of time:

'I'm sorry . . . I'm really rather certain that at no point did I
mention Latvia, or clogs, although I do recall that I said that
the elder brother came home and heard the sound of music
and dancing . . . so, yes, there was dancing involved . . .'

They look bewildered, and then unite in being adamant.

'No, we both looked at each other in amazement when you
mentioned Latvian folk traditions. The way they tie those
little bells to their ankles and small children throw daffodils
and then they gather afterwards to eat a thick noodle-based
soup, a little like Russian borscht . . .'

I give up, and wish them well in Latvia. Sometimes, when
I'm credited for something that I have never said, I don't
even try to protest, as happened once when two ladies
approached me.

'Jeff, thanks so much for what you said about prayer in your
sermon a few weeks ago . . .'

I knew I definitely had not mentioned prayer recently, but
decided that, hey, it wasn't worth putting up a fight.

'You're very welcome', I smiled benevolently, 'I'm so glad you found it useful. It's so gratifying when a sermon helps switch the light on and . . .'

'Hold on!' interrupts the accompanying lady. 'I've just remembered, Wilma. It wasn't Jeff who spoke about prayer. It was John, that guest speaker from Birmingham. He's the one who talked about hanging in there when all seems lost.'

'Of course, you're right', exclaims Wilma. Then both ladies stare at me with bewildered fascination and pity, feeling the need to urgently pray for the preacher who apparently is so desperate for encouragement, he'll take credit for other people's sermons.

Back to knowing the will of God. Someone said that if I didn't have peace, then I wasn't in the will of God. They said that peace would act like an umpire in a cricket match, confirming my decisions. This had the emotional effect of receiving the delivery of a fast bowler in the place where it most hurts. I was so terrified of making a mistake, peace was impossible, so I had no peace because I had no peace, if you get my drift. By the way, that verse about peace being like an umpire has nothing to do with guidance. It's about relationships in the church, and how the Holy Spirit wants to help us to avoid murdering each other. It's a verse that should surely be planted on the communal refrigerator of every Christian community, like Scargill.

I was especially traumatised by the impossible notion that there was only one specially selected person that I could marry: the One. Of course, this is tosh. The Bible says nothing to suggest that. It is refreshingly earthy. Paul effectively says, 'If you want to have sex, get married', which is blunt. If there is only one person we can marry, then what happens when there's a divorce, or a partner dies? If we marry again, is that person the perfect 'One', version 2, kept waiting in the wings until needed?

It seems to me that simply making ourselves available to God is the key to all this stuff. We offer ourselves to him, and trying to mean what we say as we do so. And we need to grow up and learn how to make good decisions. The Bible says a lot more about growing in wisdom (learning from life) than revelation (hearing from God).

Oops. I've written all this but I've just remembered that you suggested that I should lay a fleece before replying. Amazingly, when I went to Sainsbury's today, I bumped into a bassoon-playing Japanese sumo wrestler who had one foot in a bowl of custard. The only problem is that the actual fleece that I laid was that my mother-in-law would smile at me if it was right that I try to respond to your question. She didn't, mainly because I'm currently 5,489 miles from her.

But I decided to write anyway.

Hope it's vaguely helpful.

　　　　With love,
　　　　　　Jeff

PS: Do you want me to send you a bucket of slightly sweaty Sumo custard?

ELEVEN

Hi Jeff,

Curiously enough, I currently have exactly the amount of Tesco's Slightly Sweaty Sumo Custard that I need – for at least another week. Every little disgusts. But thanks for your kind offer. Thanks also for responding to my question about guidance. You are definitely not alone in that early experience of neurotic concern about 'getting it right'. I suppose this is yet another example of those disturbing areas of Christian teaching and experience where superstition and faith overlap in ways that are strange, and sometimes quite damaging.

By the way, your instructive and entertaining comments about Gideon and his fleece reminded me of a seminar I took part in years ago at Greenbelt, the Christian festival held at the end of August every year. The seminar was entitled 'How far can we go with humour?', or something along those lines, and it was very well attended. That was hardly surprising when you consider that the participants included Stewart Henderson, a fine poet and very funny public speaker, and Mike Yaconelli, American founder of the famous Christian satirical magazine, *The Wittenberg Door*.

I have no idea what the creators and organisers of this event were expecting from us. I suppose it is just possible

that they were anticipating some kind of serious, constructive discussion, but I suspected (and so would you
have done, Jeff) that they were actually hoping we would
use it as an excuse to tell all the jokes that we hadn't been
able to get away with in most church situations. Well,
whatever anyone expected, that's what we ended up
doing, much to the delight of the hundreds of palpably
non-serious Greenbelters who packed the tent that morning. Hilarity reigned, and the line between acceptable and
unacceptable was blurred and smudged, if not rubbed
out altogether.

One small, not very distinguished contribution from
me was a new definition for 'laying a fleece'.

'Might not this phrase', I suggested, 'describe the activity envisaged by lustful rams on a Friday night?'

You'd be able to tell I write humour for a living, even if
you didn't already know, wouldn't you, Jeff?

This business of blurring lines is interesting. I don't
know if you ever read *The Sunday Times Magazine*, but it
recently featured a piece on the resurgence of a garish and
blatantly decadent life-style that was once familiar in the
major cities of Germany. The article began with a rather
ominous suggestion that the contents were unsuitable or
inappropriate for children, and went on to describe parties and orgies where complicated acts of group sex are
performed by several people at the same time in just
about every permutation you can imagine. Photographs
accompanying the text depicted some of the folk
involved, most of them dressed (more or less) in vividly
coloured clothes, and made up with a sort of devilish
artistry.

I was interested to note my reaction. I have never found
the idea of orgies erotic or attractive in any way, but is this
a sound Christian and moral perspective, or is it simply a

reflection of the way I am made? For instance, my partici-
pation in the complicated conjunction of five or six bodies
in all manner of sexual linkings (rather like those Stickle
Bricks models my children used to make) would be
impossible. I simply cannot multi-task. I really can't. Not
in any circumstances. And how is the thing organised?
Does someone sketch the shapes and angles, give out
copies for individual study before it begins, and then
announce 'Positions everybody!' and blow a whistle?

Then there is the boredom factor. I just know that after
a few minutes of full-on hideous revelry and moral abandonment, I would be offering to make us all a lovely cup
of tea, and suggesting that we settle down in front of the
DVD player to enjoy a nice long episode of *Poirot*. That
would put a bit of a dent in the orgy ethos, don't you
think? The other Stickle Bricks wouldn't like me.

I don't know how these people do it, Jeff. Honestly,
their Bacchanalian stamina bewilders me. They must
work out at the gym daily and determinedly in order to
get through one of these all-night sessions without having to retire with cramp or respiratory discomfort.
Twenty minutes of charades wears me out.

I suppose the serious point I'm lurching towards is that
none of us can take a personal pride in embracing ethical
viewpoints that line up with Christian doctrine, especially
when the specific moral turpitude in question doesn't
appeal to us anyway. The kind of scenes described in that
article appal and bewilder me in equal measure, but my
feeble hope is that, as a follower of Jesus, I would avoid
such excesses like the plague, even if they were all that my
heart and body desired. What do you think, Jeff? Any
interesting confessions to offer?

Continuing the theme of blurred lines and the media, I
got myself into a state of distress and confusion a couple

of Sundays ago, as I watched a television debate on the subject: 'Is there any evidence for the existence of God?' Those involved in the discussion included men and women representing a variety of faiths, and an equal number of people, scientists and others, who argued that there is no logical, scientific or provable evidence to support the claim that God exists. The discussion became quite lively, especially as one member of the pro-God squad, a rather impressive fellow, was himself an acclaimed scientist. Also on this side of the argument was a famously liberal Anglican clergyman, who seemed to disappear into the folds of his own theologically twisted knickers every time he opened his mouth.

The anti-God gang spoke a great deal about something called 'truth', a phenomenon that appeared to exist, in their minds at least, only in the same way that a spark struck from flint is true because it can be seen, and experienced through touch. It was a dismal perspective. Two questions rolled around my mind. Is there no other kind of truth? Are we genuinely that impoverished? Some of the truth-seekers spoke well, but most of them viewed their believing opponents with the same expression of mild scorn and pity in their eyes as the judges on *Britain's Got Talent* when Paul Potts shambled to centre-stage and prepared to give the performance of his life.

Why was I in a state of distress? To tell you the truth, Jeff, I think it was because my second question concerned the fact that I hadn't the faintest idea what I would have said if I had been in that studio. How could someone who's been writing and speaking about the Christian faith for nearly thirty years feel so dumb and indecisive?

Things changed for the better towards the end of the programme, when a Christian lady began to speak about the way in which her faith, and especially her relationship with Jesus, had supported and sustained her through a tragic, agonising phase in her life. The sardonic smiles faded. This lady wasn't arguing. She wasn't discussing. She was simply talking about something that was true and powerful inside her. Jeff, I just loved her for helping me rediscover the essential dividing line between Christianity and Christ. The first doesn't do anything, and it wins no arguments. The second is everything because it isn't it, it's him. He just happens.

I've said it before and I'll say it again – faith is weird.

Cheers, Jeff.

Adrian

TWELVE

Dear Adrian,

I'm intrigued (and perhaps a little relieved) to hear that you wouldn't want to participate in an orgy, mainly because your lack of flexibility would prevent you from performing the required contortions, and you lack the necessary physical stamina for such extended aerobic activity. It would be excruciatingly embarrassing, wouldn't it, if slap bang (forgive the terminology) in the middle of a Roman style debauch, you were forced to ask for a brief time out so that you could catch your breath or take a nap? Worse still, it would be awful to pull a muscle in the middle of the proceedings, or be leaping around yelling that you've got cramped calves while everyone else carried on?

I'm with you: a good round of charades, or better still, Scrabble has a greater capacity to entertain and tends to make one less vulnerable to unspeakable diseases. Besides that, faced with an invitation to an orgy, I'd worry about a couple of my organs.

I'm not sure my ears could cope. The sound of laughter coming from the other participants would be deafening, a rising cacophony of disdain that would greet my taking my kit off. Actually, the more I think about it (and I confess that

I have not spent much time pondering my potential response to such an invitation, not having lived as either a hedonistic German or an ancient Roman) the more I conclude that group sex would be utterly vile. There's the aesthetic challenge of all of that heaving, raw, un-airbrushed flesh: it would be such a revolting sight. Sex is often packaged in the thin veil of unreality. Super models who use seduction to sell clothes, perfume or even watches aren't shown with spidery varicose veins, hairy nostrils, or cellulite marbled flesh. Sex scenes in films don't usually include actors with flaws. Normal physical imperfections are Photoshopped away, and the film industry employs people to act as stand-ins when the starlet hasn't got a pert enough bottom (imagine being a pert bottom stand in, Adrian? Great work if you can get it . . .).

But an orgy would reveal the cold, frequently unpalatable truth: bellies droop, fat bulges, breasts flop, and the male member is a very ugly sight, and I'm not talking about a chap who votes in the House of Commons.

Let's face it, much of the allure of sexuality is based on the cover-up, in the tantalizing notion of what *might* lie beneath, rather than the full-on disappointing sight of what actually *does*. I discovered this recently during a trip to the Caribbean. Parked on the impossibly white sand of what we thought was the best beach in the region, we were unaware that we were on the border between a clothed and a nudist beach, where a few people were intent on flashing their full frontals and from all angles. Initially unaware and happily clothed in my Bermuda shorts, I swam for a while, and then dived beneath the turquoise water to inspect what looked like a starfish. When I resurfaced, I was stunned to see that a totally naked woman was marching towards me. Yikes. Had I drowned and gone to heaven? Was I in some kind of

Islamic afterlife packed with beautiful virgins who for some reason loved swimming?

As the naked lady struggled past me, against the current, I kept my eyes straight ahead, but was conscious that I had turned beetroot with embarrassment. This was irrational, since I was the one with the clothes on.

Things were to get a little more awkward back on the beach. Lining up for a lunchtime snack, I was appalled to find totally naked men in the queue at the beach BBQ. The chap in front of me, also clothed in shorts, turned and whispered with a wry smile, 'It's enough to put you off hot dogs for life, isn't it?'

Indeed it was and is. I ordered a cheeseburger, and hoped and prayed that the naked chaps wouldn't get too close to the grill. Then sin overtook me, and I prayed that the naked chaps *would* get too close to the grill.

But that day I learned that most of those who take all their clothes off in public shouldn't. All of that wobbly flesh could perhaps cure a sex addict in a heartbeat. Reality can be very ugly indeed.

Now all of this talk about the stark nature of reality leads me away from the subject of sex (aren't you relieved?) to that which you and I both try to do, being honest. Yes, we love to laugh, but I know that much of our humour is purposeful, because we want to be real and tell the truth. It still stuns me that some Christians find straight talking surprising. Perhaps part of the reason is that we'd prefer our Christianity to be sanitised and airbrushed, where prayers are always answered. Too much real talk about the sweaty ugliness of life in general, and the Christian life in particular, makes some people uncomfortable. I'm so glad to be in your company, and that of other cherished friends, who want the truth, even when it is unpalatable. Tarted-up Christianity is a con, a deviation, and I want no part of it. Count me out of an orgy – and I'll pass when it comes to sham faith too.

Before we finally leave your musings about orgies (you need to get out more), may I say I was intrigued about whether our choices are based on moral faithfulness or personal preference. I suppose the truth is that both are involved. I am always unfailingly victorious when tempted to play the bassoon, skydive, play rugby, or get obsessive about basket weaving, because I have absolutely no desire to do any of those things.

Much of the time we don't do bad things simply because we don't want to. But even then, there might be something – or someone – involved beneath the surface of those decisions.

I'll try to explain. There have been times when I have been genuinely tempted to do something that presented itself as being deeply delicious, but wrong. I had the opportunity to indulge myself and dive, head first, into a sea of salaciousness. But then something strange happened . . .

It was like a hunger, rising up from deep inside me somewhere, an urge to do what was right. Not just because it was right, not because I was being shunted down rigid train lines of guilt or conscience, but because I genuinely wanted to do what was right more than I wanted to do what was wrong. I don't think I'm over-spiritualizing things when I say that I believe this was God at work in me. Not just in that moment of crisis, but working slowly and steadily each day, as he turns me into a person who resembles Jesus, instinctively wanting to do what is right and good. Isn't transformation about that? I wish I could say this has happened a lot more than it has, but I would be straying into unreality again. But I've been grateful for the episodes when I discovered I was not the person I thought I was, or even who I thought I'd be. Grace, somehow, in some way, had made me different. What do you think? Does this make sense?

I'll sign off now, although I'd like to come back to that moment when you watched the programme about reasons not to believe in God, and felt completely devoid of any reasonable answers. Before we discuss that more, I wonder: what do you do when you are suddenly smitten with the awful possibility that all this Christian stuff is a load of rubbish? We've both talked about it before, so we know that it happens. My question is – what is your response when it does?

Much love as ever,
Jeff

THIRTEEN

Hi Jeff,

Well, if I wasn't enthusiastic about orgies before, I'm even less keen on the idea now. Thanks very much for the intense and intensive session of aversion therapy provided by the first part of your letter. Yes, thank God for Scrabble, the only version of a night on the tiles that we seem to manage nowadays. The Stickle Bricks people can do their own thing. I shall continue to embrace monogamy, or is it known as 'stereogamy' in this advanced technological age?

Just a final note on the subject of sex. I wrote a novel a few years ago featuring a recently widowed male character, who is seriously tempted by a very attractive woman who visits his bedroom in the middle of the night. He resists the temptation by the skin of his teeth for two reasons. One is the sheer inappropriateness of using an opportunity and a person to temporarily fill the aching gap in his life. The other is quite simply a teeth-gritted decision that being a follower of Jesus really does mean something to him, and therefore he wants to do the thing that is right just slightly more than he wants to do the thing that he believes is wrong. Once she has left the room, of course, he rocks and rages with frustration, but when the morning comes he is glad, and so is she.

I found it mind-bogglingly weird that one of the editors involved with this book felt that the scene should be changed or removed altogether, not because of the sexual content, but because, in the words of the person concerned, 'This would never happen. Readers are never going to believe any man would turn down an opportunity like that, Christian or not.'

In a way, this links in with what you were saying about truth, Jeff. 'Tarted-up' Christianity, as you termed it with your accustomed delicate touch, is very wary about encountering or seriously dealing with the things that happen when we are not firmly embedded in the safe context of intentional religious activity. For heaven's sake! If it really is impossible for a Christian to withstand powerful sexual temptation, let's just fold up our stupid, meaningless little pseudo-Christian tents and creep away to somewhere where expectations are less demanding. And you know I'm not saying that it's easy to stay clean, Jeff. I'm saying that unless we face these things head-on and bring the Holy Spirit right into the centre of the discussion, we're likely to end up playing games and wasting our time. The Bible says we will never be tempted beyond our power to resist. Is that true, or is it a load of rubbish?

And yet, this path of openness is a tricky one to tread in some ways, especially for those of us who have been fed with religious patterns and mantras like breast milk. Refusing this kind of thin nourishment (excuse my typically violent swings of metaphor) is like dropping the cloak that has hitherto identified us as believers. Underneath we may be thin and naked, but at least there is a possibility that we shall be clothed by God instead of the proprietors of some Christian Primark in a side road off the high street. Assuming we have new spiritual trousers, or any trousers at all if it comes to that, perhaps he will offer us the Belt of Truth to stop them from falling down. Do we want to wear this blessed belt? Do you, Jeff? Do I? I think I do, but it scares me.

Offering some suffering soul a verse of Scripture unsupported by love or substance is about as useful as giving pictures of a blazing fire to someone with cold hands. That's true.

Not many people are healed through prayer or by the laying on of hands. A few are. That's true.

We are still largely a church of consumers, leaning towards comfort and rationalisation of inaction, as far as obedience to God is concerned. That's true.

Many church communities are far more passionately opposed to homosexuality than they are to greed, in a world where huge numbers of children die of starvation and disease every single day, all over the planet. That's definitely true.

And all this brings me to your final question. What is my response when I am suddenly hit by a fear that Christianity is a load of nonsense? We keep coming back to this subject, don't we, Jeff? The 'D' word. Doubt. Discussion topics in our letters seem to have a sort of spiral progression, round and round and round, but hopefully with a little bit of accretion or upward movement from time to time.

I can guess why you brought this up. You're recalling that evening when you and I invited questions from the audience, and someone wanted to know our greatest fear. I told the truth. Only just. My greatest fear was and is that the faith I have written and spoken about for nearly thirty years has no basis in reality. A strange, gently rustling frisson passed through the audience when I made that statement. I think it was a murmur of identification. Nearly all of them must have faced the same conundrum as me at one time or another.

Jesus makes me laugh and cry and make strange decisions and travel huge distances and experience remarkable joy as well as deep despair. How can that set of experiences be accompanied by intermittent bouts of total doubt, rather like being trapped in a tunnel with no light at either end or, as G.K. Chesterton put it, in a maze with no centre? I have no very convincing answer to that question, and I shan't bother to repeat the bog-standard explanations that are usually ladled out. You know them as well as I do, Jeff. What I can say is that faith and doubt seem to be twins, joined at birth. In some inexplicable way it seems as difficult and as pointless to rend them apart as it is to separate the wheat and tares in the famous Gospel parable.

How do I respond when I am hit by that fear? I am devastated. I am intrigued by my own devastation simply because I am always intrigued by every single thing that happens. I am filled with unhappiness and a deep claustrophobic fear. It can get very bad sometimes. It can end with me sadly exiting the residence of my faith and all its ridiculous paraphernalia, carefully shutting the door behind me as I go. At this point, invariably, I hear the faintest of urgent whispers from somewhere inside me.

'Can I come?'

And we leave together. The interesting thing is that I never need anything that I've left behind.

Lots of love to you,
Adrian

FOURTEEN

Dear Adrian,

Thanks for your last letter, and especially for not answering my question about doubt – at least not answering it in the way that most Christians seem to approach the thorny issue. I knew that I didn't have to fear that you'd give me five ways to vanquish doubt, each proven method beginning with the same letter. When people try those little snappy answers on me, I find myself plunged into deeper doubt. Their natty alliteration codifies faith in a way that makes Christianity about as attractive as a slab of pork a few days past its sell-by date. As a preacher, I often find myself niggled by doubt when reading commentaries, which I love and hate in almost equal measure. Sometimes, when erudite scholars analyze and alliterate, they leave me cold. Even the most beautiful human body is made ugly by dissection.

I note your comment about circular conversations, but I'd like to ponder the issue of doubt for just a moment more, if I may, because, for me, doubt is a mosquito that I can never quite kill. If your last letter is to be believed, I never will successfully swat it this side of the New Jerusalem. I apologise in advance because I'm going to get very serious for a few paragraphs, and I promise that, once I get this off my chest, I'll lighten up. Honest.

Most of the time, doubt rumbles rather than roars, the vaguest trembling of the ground that I stand on. Distant, irritating, troubling even, but not turbulent enough to create an earthquake that Richter would be interested in. But every now and again I have a full-on faith attack, which threatens to wipe out everything I believe in.

I use this term faith attack because I am familiar with panic attacks. Have you ever had one of those? Pass it up if you're ever offered one. They often hit me last thing at night, when the whirring cogs of my mind are refusing to slow down, and suddenly a quite irrational thought strikes and grips my soul with a knuckle-white fist. I can feel like I'm drowning in the dark.

Recently I've had a few attacks when I think about my mother, who is battling with the late stages of dementia. It fills me with unspeakable terror, the thought of becoming a prisoner in a mind that has become a confused, bewildering labyrinth, where frightening creatures crouch in the shadows, where we are torn from our memories and our nearest and dearest, all with a sense that it is going to get much, much worse. I cannot contemplate the thought of it without breaking into a sweat. Sometimes these panic attacks get so bad, I have to get up and put the light on, and even walk around the house for a while, to prise myself from their clammy claws. I refer to these experiences because they are utterly debilitating. And so it is with faith attacks. They strike without warning, and are triggered by such random happenings.

Sometimes it's the superstitious old wives' tale statements that Christians produce that make Christianity suddenly implausible, and for a moment the whole faith construct seems as rickety as a coffee table made by a first year in the woodwork class. *You can't out give God*, they say. Really? Then why not give every penny you possess and become utterly destitute (at least temporarily), if that's really true? *God is in control*. No, he's not, at least not in the sense that everything that happens is because he wants it to. If that's not the case, why do we pray 'Your kingdom come, your will be done', if in a bizarre *que sera sera* kind of way, everything that happens is because God wills it? *Things have gone wrong, so you must be doing something right* is often trotted out by those who have an excessive view of spiritual warfare that may mean that Satan is, in fact, camping in my bathroom. *I'm healed* says the person who very obviously isn't: they think that they're letting the side down if they don't.

Or it can come, as it did yesterday, when I hear about the Christian leader who has dumped his wife and children, married one of his young assistants and is now back on the road again – leading family events. Cue faith attack. Suddenly, I feel like a First World War soldier who has gone over the top in the Somme, only to discover that he has left his gun behind.

Or it can be a brush with mortality, which I had just this week, with the death of a very close relative who was one of the best parts of my growing up. When I heard the news, the Easter message seemed empty. I didn't feel comforted – I felt that I was desperately trying to be hopeful, but it wasn't working. The possibility of there being another place, somewhere else in the Universe, that she had travelled to – it all seemed about as likely as the Easter bunny or Santa, wishful thinking. My faith was not rammed by a weighty locomotive filled with brilliant New Atheist arguments, but shattered by the hint of a satanic snigger.

Okay, enough of this already. I just wanted to tell someone about these faith attacks, in the hope that if anyone else gets to read our letters, they at least will know that they're not alone. As to how I deal with them, I take the same approach as I do with panic attacks. I walk around, put the kettle on, and wait for them to pass. And then I decide to believe again that I am not forsaken.

It seems to me that faith gives us the ability to rise above the default human condition of feeling abandoned and alone. If I had choreographed the Easter events, I wouldn't have had Jesus yelling, 'My God, my God, why have you forsaken me?' as one of his last statements. That didn't sound too good, did it, coming from the One who had announced that he and his Father were one? Very bad as a parting shot, I'd say. I wonder what those who heard him say that made of it, without a team of forensic commentators standing by to explain it all in three points of alliterated sermonic clarity.

Perhaps Jesus was fully embracing the basic human condition: lostness, bewilderment, and a feeling that heaven is ignoring us much of the time. On the cross, not only was he challenging the power of death, but identifying with us in the experience of hopeless, desolate life. Three days later, he rose to let us know, once and for all, that we are not abandoned or left destitute.

And that leads me to another 'parting shot' from Jesus. Before dying, he said 'You've forsaken me.' Before ascending, he promised, 'I'll never leave you.' And faith leads me to believe that this statement is true. But my occasional faith attacks and 'Where are you God?' crises don't mean that I'm a rubbish Christian, just another human trying to get synchronised with what is true, rather than what I fear.

Much love,
Jeff

FIFTEEN

Hi Jeff,

Four things occurred to me as I read your last letter. The first might seem trivial, but I don't think it is. It was inspired by your comment about getting up and putting the kettle on in the middle of the night when your peace is destroyed by panic attacks.

Tea.

A cup of tea.

Two cups of tea.

A large mug of tea.

A large mug of tea made by someone else.

Let's tell it how it is, Jeff. Bible verses may occasionally coax or comfort. Prayer can result in temporary relief. Praise and worship have been known to have a faintly distracting effect. The fellowship of our brothers and sisters might numb the pain just a little. Preaching reminds us that there is more than one kind of suffering. But none of these can rival the sheer genius of tea.

Tea demands no relationship, no straining faith in someone or something that is achingly difficult to properly perceive or comprehend, no complex investment in rhymes and mimes and special times that seem sillier the more you look at them, and no grindingly persistent requirement that we express certainty about concepts that are as impenetrable and bewildering as a set of flat-pack instructions in Dutch. Those who cast out devils are intermittently successful, but tea? Tea always delivers.

Last Sunday, after a full-on weekend of hosting and teaching at the place where we work, Bridget and I sat at home in a state of near-terminal weariness, staring at each other and the walls as we dribbled and gibbered like junkies because we had no tea. The village shop was closed. There was no one in next door. It was too icy and dangerous to drive the five miles between us and the Spar shop in Grassington. It was agonizing. We didn't want alcohol, we didn't want coffee, we didn't want milk, we didn't want fruit juice, we didn't want anything except tea, and there was none. Why bother to exist at all in such a bleak and pointless world? We crept miserably to bed in the end, all too conscious that the early part of the following day would be a tea-forsaken pit of utter despair.

At eight o'clock in the morning – joy of joys! Bridget triumphantly placed a mug of hot tea on the cupboard beside my bed. Not a miracle, but an inspiration. My endlessly ingenious wife had remembered a little china pot down in the kitchen that contained the used teabags left over from two or three days ago. They worked! God be praised! They made two perfectly good cups of tea. We were saved. Hallelujah!

So, Jeff, now I say to God, 'Am I being too flippant about this? Dissing all the spiritual stuff and praising tea to the heavens?'

And he (as far as he says anything) replies, 'Good heavens, no, I'm rather proud of tea actually. My idea, you know. Elijah, Jeff Lucas, all sorts of people need a spot of refreshment when they wake up and panic in the middle of the night. I've been doing it for years.'

So, that was the tea. Sorry, went on about that a bit, didn't I? Probably a symptom of my growing belief that abstract spirituality is an impressively rainbow-hued herring in comparison with God-given delights that actually help.

Then there was your reference to feeling like a Somme warrior clambering out of the trench to go into battle, only to find you've left your gun behind. Interesting. That must be roughly what they said about Jesus when he stood in front of Pilate and refused to open his mouth. He'd already told Peter to put his sword away, and twelve legions of angels had been sent muttering darkly back to barracks. I wonder what the bystanders said?

'Look at that idiot! Facing torture and death without a word or a weapon to defend himself.'

What kind of gun are we supposed to be armed with as we go over the top, Jeff? That's not a rhetorical question. I don't know what the answer is. All I know for sure is that I'm not allowed to be in charge of the armoury. Do you think our most powerful weapon might be that we are doing the right thing in the right place? The rest is not our decision. It's not fair, is it, Jeff? Ironic or what? We Christians have to surrender to our own Commander before we get permission to face the enemy. Who'd be a follower of Jesus, eh?

The third thing that occurred to me is something that I think I've written about before. It's a (to me) horribly graphic illustration of the problems that both of us face as we struggle through the lifetime cycle of belief and doubt and following and fading and nearly giving up and picking ourselves up and starting again. There was a cartoon on the wall of our kitchen when the children were small. I hated it really, and I still don't know why I left it up there. It was a drawing of a hamster wheel. Inside the wheel,

Daddy hamster is paddling away furiously, closely followed by Mummy hamster and their two youngsters. The
little boy hamster is speaking:

'Are we there yet, Daddy?'

The shadow of the fear of failed fatherhood sinks into
my very soul even as I write these words. Where was I
taking my helpless, trusting kids? How was I in any way
equipped to lead them through the early years of their
lives? What would they think of me when they discovered that I was more frightened of the journey than they
were? Every time I looked at that picture on the wall, it
was like seeing my ongoing nightmare in the mirror.

The way things have actually worked out is another
story, of course, a wider range of emotions and experiences than I could ever have imagined. I wouldn't have
missed it for the world. But, as I say, that's another very
long story. I mention my old cartoon here because the
darkness and panic that you describe (and I have known
them myself) are not about the father, but about the
anguish of the son or daughter. Are we on some kind of
wheel? Does anyone really know where we're supposed
to be going? If we paddle away frantically as hard as we
can, will somebody be pleased with our efforts and eventually say, 'Yes, you have arrived. It wasn't a wheel.
We've all arrived. Following was worth it. Thank you.
You can rest now.'

And the fourth thing? I've never done this before. I
want to pray in this letter. I want to pray for you, Jeff, and
for me and for any others who might read these words.

Father, we so want you to really and truly be our
Father, leading us and holding on to us, and joining us for
a cup of tea now and then in the middle of the night, and
letting us help, and understanding when it all goes
wrong, and sharing your passionate ambitions with us,

and letting us see just a glimpse of the hurt that sears your divine soul when the crucified Jesus is rejected yet again by the people for whom he died, and helping us to understand that only a little bit of the staggering truth can become visible in this world, and working for us without a pause behind the scenes. We surrender. Hold us. Send us out to battle. Thanks. Amen.

God bless you, Jeff. Lots of adventures ahead.

Love, Adrian

SIXTEEN

Dear Adrian,

I was relieved to read your last letter, in which you came close to worshipping the most luscious invention that is tea. I too am smitten with the beautiful drink, and at times find myself feeling ransomed, healed, restored and forgiven, and all because of the wonder created by Tetley or Typhoo. Even as I write this, a voluminous mug is parked by my computer, which is dangerous but necessary. Years ago, at Spring Harvest, my habit of drinking tea while working on my computer caused technological meltdown, literally. Attempting to make a cup of tea in the cramped chalet, I stumbled and poured the contents of a boiling kettle into the keyboard of my laptop, which screamed, died, and refused to work for a fortnight. I also screamed, wanted to die, and had great difficulty in getting any work done. Despite this scalding incident, my love for tea remains unabated.

But my love affair with tea creates some difficulties. Living much of the time in America, I often pine for a genuine cup of British char (any idea why we call it char, by the way?).

Tea is served here, but most often it comes as iced tea: a blasphemous beverage. The notion of plopping ice cubes into what should be hot tea fills me with horror. It's just wrong, like serving deep-fried steak and kidney pies. I have ordered hot tea in a few American restaurants, but it usually comes served in a container that looks suspiciously like a hospital specimen bottle. One sip of the contents confirms that it actually *is* a hospital specimen bottle.

Your letter, where you enthusiastically testified to the renewing power of tea, reminded me that we tend to think that our 'spiritual' lives are helped by 'spiritual' things, like worship, prayer, and Bible study, especially if that Bible study doesn't land us in Leviticus or the minor prophets. Of course, God is not interested in our 'spiritual lives', but our lives. He doesn't aspire to make us more spiritual, but more authentically human, with Jesus as the model of true humanness, and the Holy Spirit working away in us to actually make us into something like Christ. After all, God invented the human condition. Some Christians give me the impression that they're trying to get away from being human so that they can be something else. Perhaps we've taken the word that the English Bible translates 'flesh' and used that to fuel an irrational scrambling to be other than human. But human is what God wants us to be. As we stumble our way through the best and worst of times, slowly, painfully becoming healthily human, our potential is huge. That makes the pathetic bleat that 'We're only human' something of an oxymoron.

That's why I was saddened to hear that your editor/publisher wanted to delete the episode in your book, when that lonely character resisted the welcome opportunity to hop into bed with someone he wasn't married to. To wrinkle our noses in disbelief at such goodness and faithfulness surely means that we don't believe in this Christian message. We are being shaped into Jesus-like people, and so of course we can make the right choices. If we surrender to the idea that this is unrealistic, then I agree – let's abandon this whole Christian idea as nothing more than that – a pleasant, irrelevant notion. As we travel, and sometimes trudge along the road with Jesus, we find he has ingenious ways to strengthen us, especially when we find ourselves on the steeper, uphill paths, and it feels like dusk is closing in fast. Tea is part of his blessing toolkit, which also includes unexpected smiles from strangers, salty air on the beach, steak cooked medium–well, the fragrance of flowers, crispy Yorkshire pudding, elderly people who are frail and often lonely but can still laugh, crackling log fires in Sussex, long evenings spent nattering about nothing much with friends and, in your case, custard. When we narrow 'blessing' down to goose bumps when a worship song goes up a key, surely we hem God in with our small expectations.

Of course God uses people as well as tea. Recently I've found myself being grateful for people that I've met. Just bumping into them has brought sunshine to my soul. Their sometimes strange beauty has moved me, challenged me, inspired me to continue the trek. Just as Paul the Apostle spoke of being refreshed by the coming of a friend (2 Tim. 1:16) so I've encountered some people lately whose words, smiles, and stories have been like clear cold water to my sometimes parched soul. Sunshine and clear cold water. Sorry for the mixed metaphors.

We both have plenty of stories about some of the very strange people that we encounter in our travels through Planet Church – and every time I think I've met the Olympic champion of difficult Christians, another one pops up and snatches the gold medal. A few weeks ago a chap sternly told me that my preaching was not to his taste, which made me feel like a pizza. Not that I have to be liked by everyone, although it would be preferable.

But here's the lovely truth: the unkind, awkward and permanently offended souls are the minority. I meet far more humble, hilarious, beautiful followers of Jesus who make the ranters and the furrowed brow brigade the exception rather than the majority. And when I meet them, they're like a cup of tea. Refreshing. Invigorating. Surprising. Self-sacrificing (okay, the tea analogy runs out with self-sacrificing).

One of them is called Shotgun. His real name is James, but for years, everyone has called him Shotgun. I have no idea why. He lives in Oklahoma, which may provide a clue. Shotgun is 92 years old now, and lived most of his life without wanting Jesus to be part of it. When he was twelve, he attended one of those country revival meetings where everyone gets excited, speaks in tongues, and worship is loud and frenzied. Shotgun was thinking about becoming a Christian, and so went down to the front of the tent during what's called the altar call. Lots of excited people gathered around him and prayed for half an hour. During that long thirty minutes, Shotgun told God that if he was real, then he'd like to meet him. Nothing happened. The prayer team got louder, but God stayed silent. Shotgun describes the experience as being one of the most disappointing of his life. He walked out of the tent and decided to ignore God for the rest of his days, and so he lived the rough and ready life of an oil worker, often drunk, getting into brawls, and occasionally thrown in jail.

It went on that way for some seven decades. His wife was the love of his life, and so, when they were both in their mid-eighties and she announced that she thought they should go to church, he agreed. A short while later, Shotgun's wife became very ill. He was granted a rare privilege. One night, they lay awake for most of the night, reminiscing, reviewing their lives together, whispering words of love. In the morning, he awoke to find that she was not in their bed. She had got up, made her way to their lounge, where he found her, sitting up against the couch, quite dead. Six months later, Shotgun walked into his pastor's study, and said, 'I'm ready.' They knelt down together on the floor, and Shotgun asked Jesus if they could reconnect.

Reconnect they have, and the result is beautiful. I see Shotgun about once a year, when I visit the church that he's part of. He's always tearful and tender. Everyone in his church loves him, he arrives for services early, and makes them coffee (there you are, Adrian, there's the blessing of hot drinks again). He's full of questions, and shows a rare ability, for a man of his age, to grow and change. I saw him this week. He's had a car accident, and is walking around with his arm in a sling, with a gigantic cube of yellow foam to protect his forearm. He looked like a walking advertisement for Cheddar cheese. But more noticeable than the cheese block, as always, is his kindness, which is quietly outstanding. Once again, I am refreshed today because of dear Shotgun. Hot drinks and kindness. A great combination.

Okay, enough already. My mug is empty. I'll put the kettle on. Why don't you and Bridget come over?

With love,
Jeff

SEVENTEEN

Hi Jeff,

We'd love to come for tea, Jeff, but five thousand miles is a bit of a long haul. By the way, I gather that tea is called 'char' because it first originated from a Chinese term 'tcha' which refers to Chinese monks, who were the first people to grow tea. I knew that already, of course. Just needed to check it with Google . . .

Aren't you lucky to know Shotgun? I thought about him today. Someone wrote to me about 'extremeness'. This fellow had just finished reading one of my books with the title, *Jesus – Safe, Tender and Extreme*, and wondered how I felt about the suggestion that extremeness might be the only true way to safety. It's easy to find yourself sinking into a pointlessly abstract swamp with discussions like these, but the question dovetailed into something I have been wrestling with for some time. You see, I broadly agree with this proposition, but the essential nature of that extremeness is something of a tantalizing mystery to me.

There is a hard thing about being or continuing to be a Christian. Hard to say, hard to write, even hard to think coherently. There seems to be a place of transference, rather like an airlock, where movement into unquestionable safety and certainty can be facilitated but, bewilderingly and frighteningly, cannot be guaranteed. We cannot logic or love or manipulate ourselves into this other world because the change is like a change in the way we breathe and see and balance. It is governed by alien rules and differences in platforms of security that we simply will not understand until we are there. Some modern theologians suggest that if we have not understood that Jesus sometimes doubted his own divinity, we have not understood the Gospels at all.

Perhaps Jesus himself needed to tremulously enter that fearsome no-man's-land in order to discover that there really was a strange peace awaiting him on the other side. During that transition he cried out in anguish to his father that he not only felt, but indeed was forsaken. No way back from the blessed, blasted airlock, and the possibility of nothing at all on the other side. Now that's extreme. Do I want to do it? Is it the way to safety? Dunno. How about you?

I guess that, for Shotgun, the major airlock in his life has appeared as a result of the death of his wife, and it constitutes a decision to take a punt at surviving in a world of tenderness and tears, where Jesus leads him on and the future is not nearly as important as the present. Love to meet him one of these days.

A strange moment the other evening, Jeff. We were at home chatting with a small group of people, and one of them said, I suppose as a sort of discussion starter, the following words.

'Where do we all think we'll be in fifteen years from now?'

The impact of this question didn't really hit me at first, but I saw Bridget's eyebrows shoot up, and after a moment or two I understood why. Three out of our four visitors were under twenty-five, and the one who had asked the question is, I guess, somewhere in his forties. Bridget and I are hovering in our mid-sixties. Just to labour the point, in fifteen years' time the chap who asked that question will still be younger than we are now. The others will only be in their mid-thirties. Bridget and I will be zimmering unsteadily into the eighth decade of our lives, assuming that we last that long.

A few years ago I was travelling on a bus from Taunton in Somerset to Lynton in Devon, a trip that takes just under a year. During one stage of my journey I found myself eavesdropping shamelessly on a conversation between two young people sitting on the seats in front of mine. The male half of the sketch, a somewhat bovine young man of about nineteen, had been moaning wearily about everything under the sun ever since the bus had pulled out of Bridgewater. His companion, a rather pretty, dark-haired girl of similar age, seemed less than invigorated by the company of this gloom merchant.

'If I was to wake up one morning and suddenly find I was fifty,' chuntered this primitive philosopher of the Somerset and Devon Bus World, 'do you know what I'd do?'

'No I don't,' said his female friend dispassionately, 'what would you do?'

'I'd top myself.'

She seemed to brighten a little on hearing this. Perhaps she was reflecting on the fact that, if all else failed, there was a possibility of blessed relief in thirty-one years or so. I might have got that wrong, though . . .

For Bridget and I the chilling thing about the question my friend asked was the way in which it slammed a door in our faces, a heavy old impenetrable door that would exclude us from the future that these relatively young folk were talking about with such interest and animation. More sadly still, it would exclude us from the world in which our children and many of those we love would continue to experience the light and shade of life after we had left them behind. However realistic we may think we are about the realities of this world, there is bound to be a fiercely held and quite irrational conviction in our hearts that death is just an unpleasant rumour put about by thoughtless scaremongers.

As I write these words, Jeff, we are planning teaching sessions and services for Holy Week at the place where we work. Jesus only had a few days remaining at this stage of his life, and I am experiencing a strong desire to identify with this, to be right in the middle of it with him. Today I was thinking about that famous, shortest verse in the Bible.

'Jesus wept.'

This seems to have been a key point for Jesus, perhaps the moment when Jesus the Man and Jesus the God looked one another in the eye and mourned for what had been, and was bound to end in a very short time. If you don't mind I'll leave you with the reflections I've been working through and the verses from John 11 that have inspired them.

> Now a man named Lazarus was sick. He was from Bethany, the village of Mary and her sister Martha. This Mary, whose brother Lazarus now lay sick, was the same one who poured perfume on the Lord and wiped his feet with her hair. So the sisters sent word to Jesus, 'Lord, the one you love is sick.'

Given the relationship between Jesus and this little family of three, indicated in the famous account of Martha's impatience in Luke 10:38–42, and a statement 'Jesus loved Martha and her sister and Lazarus' (v5), the two sisters must have assumed that he would drop everything and come running to heal his friend.

> When he heard this, Jesus said, 'This sickness will not end in death. No, it is for God's glory so that God's Son may be glorified through it.' Jesus loved Martha and her sister and Lazarus. Yet when he heard that Lazarus was sick, he stayed where he was two more days.

Yes, he loved this family, but Jesus loved and loves everyone, surely? Why this distinction made in connection with these people in particular? Is it something to do with Jesus, the man, and the fact that there was a chemistry in that tiny community that enabled him to relax and be himself, whatever that might mean in such a singular life?

So why didn't he go?

Why does he sometimes not turn up at times when we need him most?

We all know that, however much we may love our brothers and sisters in Christ, there will always be people we 'get on with' for reasons that are to do with the way we are made. We need those relationships, as Jesus did, and clearly there is nothing wrong with them. However, sometimes we have to face, as Jesus is facing here, that at some point we shall be called to do what we see the Father doing, and this will have to take precedence over personal priorities, however passionately we may feel about the people or situations involved. As we shall see, the pain of this commitment is at the heart of Jesus' experience in these days leading up to his crucifixion.

> Then he said to his disciples, 'Let us go back to Judea.'
> 'But Rabbi,' they said, 'a short while ago the Jews tried to stone you, and yet you are going back there?'

> Jesus answered, 'Are there not twelve hours of daylight? A man who walks by day will not stumble, for he sees by this world's light. It is when he walks by night that he stumbles, for he has no light.'

What does this mean? Perhaps it's about heavenly logic again: riding the bike that goes left when you turn the handlebars to the right, and vice versa. The light or logic of the world is of little use when we walk in the light of the will of God. The logic that lies behind the way of the Holy Spirit is rarely accessible to us, even when, and if, we are quite clear about what we have to do next.

It made sense to go back and heal Lazarus, but he didn't.

It made no sense to go back and risk being stoned by the Jews, but he did.

What makes sense? God's will makes sense, but not necessarily to us.

> After he had said this, he went on to tell them, 'Our friend Lazarus has fallen asleep, but I am going there to wake him up.'
>
> His disciples replied, 'Lord, if he sleeps, he will get better.' Jesus had been speaking of his death, but his disciples thought he meant natural sleep.
>
> So then he told them plainly, 'Lazarus is dead, and for your sake I am glad I was not there, so that you may believe. But let us go to him.'

As with Jairus's daughter, Jesus sees death as a sleep, rather than an end, one of his 'silly' statements. Is this because, as Oscar Wilde suggested, he had a bold and creative imagination? Or is it a reference to the fact that, for believers, death is no more than a sleep before waking to an eternity with God?

The disciples, thick or obtuse or confused as ever, push Jesus into speaking plainly, and here we learn at least one of the reasons for his delay in travelling to see Lazarus before he died. Jesus wants his disciples to strengthen their belief in him as a time of great testing approaches. Time for action.

> Then Thomas (called Didymus) said to the rest of the disciples, 'Let us also go, that we may die with him.'
>
> On his arrival, Jesus found that Lazarus had already been in the tomb for four days. Bethany was less than two miles from Jerusalem, and many Jews had come to Martha and Mary to comfort them in the loss of their brother.

Thanks Eeyore . . .

Quite a crowd had built up, suggesting that the house and the people who lived in it were popular with lots of folk apart from Jesus. If only we were able to visit and join them all for a meal, just one cosy evening. Fascinating, eh?

> When Martha heard that Jesus was coming she went out to meet him, but Mary stayed at home.

Why did Mary stay at home? Too upset? Deeply disappointed? Unable to face the emotion that a meeting with Jesus would provoke? Was it all just too much?

> 'Lord,' Martha said to Jesus, 'if you had been here, my brother would not have died. But I know that even now God will give you whatever you ask.'
>
> Jesus said to her, 'Your brother will rise again.'
>
> Martha answered, 'I know he will rise again in the resurrection at the last day.'

Jesus said to her, 'I am the resurrection and the life. He who believes in me will live, even though he dies; and whoever lives and believes in me will never die. Do you believe this?'

'Yes, Lord,' she told him, 'I believe that you are the Christ, the Son of God, who was to come into the world.'

We cannot begin to imagine the meeting of their eyes. Martha, typically perhaps, shoots straight from the hip.

'You didn't come.'

But then, perhaps spoken with a break in her voice and unshed tears of grief and hope in her eyes:

'You're special. You are. He'll do anything you ask. You know he will.'

Will he ask?

Jesus doesn't reply directly to the unspoken question. Doggedly he lays out his priority as an obedient son of his heavenly Father. There will be resurrection for all those, including Lazarus, who believe in him. He, himself, is that resurrection. Will she affirm him in that?

She does. Priorities established? Another eye-meeting pause? Then Martha hurries off to find Mary.

And after she had said this, she went back and called her sister Mary aside. 'The Teacher is here,' she said, 'and is asking for you.'

Was he asking for her? Perhaps it just wasn't recorded. Or maybe Martha reckoned that an encounter with Mary might swing it for Lazarus. Who knows?

When Mary heard this, she got up quickly and went to him. Now Jesus had not yet entered the village, but was still at the place where Martha had met him. When the Jews who had been with Mary in the house, comforting her, noticed how quickly she got up and went out, they followed her, supposing she was going to the tomb to mourn there.

Martha had called her sister aside to tell her that Jesus had arrived, and now Mary hurried out without telling anyone where she was going. It feels like a sudden release of passion that drove her to her feet, and sent her flying to the only person who could have made a difference but, for reasons that were impossible to understand, hadn't bothered to come. What was she thinking and feeling as she rushed to see the man who had told her that she had chosen the better way, and that it would not be taken from her? He had seemed so in control, and now her brother was dead, taken from her.

When Mary reached the place where Jesus was and saw him, she fell at his feet and said, 'Lord, if you had been here, my brother would not have died.'

He'd had this twice now, this outpouring of grief and blame from two of the people he loved most in the world. Too much. All too much.

When Jesus saw her weeping, and the Jews who had come along with her also weeping, he was deeply moved in spirit and troubled. 'Where have you laid him?' he asked.
  'Come and see, Lord,' they replied.
  Jesus wept.

Why was Jesus weeping?
  People have come up with lots of different answers to that question. For me, there seems to be an aching truth at the centre of this, the shortest verse in the Bible.

Jesus was weeping because he had been obliged to do what he was told. Jesus was weeping because the divine imperative had been crystal clear. There was to be no hurried trip to Bethany in order to heal Lazarus before he died. He was weeping because, although he had made the right, obedient decision, the necessary dislocation of earth and heaven, man and God, personal love and divine love, was breaking his heart. He had tried so hard and done so very well. Now it was time to face full-on a responsibility that allowed no space for choices or decisions that would impede the salvation plan of God. But with Mary in a weeping heap at his feet, and a dark awareness in his heart of the terrible and inevitable death that awaited him, Jesus wept.

Jesus wept because all the loves and the loved ones were tearing him apart and were about to spread him piecemeal across the universe.

If Jesus wept, then perhaps we shall too if we truly want to follow his example. What will that mean, and how shall we cope with it?

Good Friday is coming. It's always coming.

God bless, Jeff

Adrian

EIGHTEEN

Hi Adrian,

Strange that you should write as you have about the question, 'Where will we be fifteen years from now?' and that lad on the bus who was terrified of reaching fifty. He has been on my mind too. Some of the visceral feelings that you've described connect with my own cluttered and confused mental meanderings of late. I've been battling with the simple reality that nothing lasts, and I'm not just talking about the 'more than rumour' ultimate junction that is death (although I'd like to explore that later, if we could. None of us are going to get out of this life alive, so it's a subject that is certainly relevant).

I've been mourning the cold fact that everything in life is temporary. Time is a relentless conveyor belt, and all of us are stuck on its juddering, ever-moving rubber lane. Onward we roll. We can scream and look in vain for a red 'Stop in the event of an emergency' button, we can complain bitterly and insist that we linger, and just take a moment more to soak up the last bit of gravy from a delicious experience, but to no avail. Right now, even as I type, the belt moves on, ushering me to the next second, to tomorrow, to next year. There is no court that will hear my desperate appeal for pause.

Life is not like a ride that I experienced once during a family holiday in Disneyland. Called 'It's a small world', we rode through a series of happy tableaux while being assaulted by some maddening music which, for some reason, settled into my memory for weeks. It was a delightful little trip, and so Kay, Kelly, Richard and I jumped off the ride at the end, and scuttled breathlessly back to the ride entrance for another turn. I think we did that six or seven times, which is probably why the irritating music is so branded on my brain. We were delighted there was no queue, nothing extra to pay, and we could take as many turns as we liked. Life, however, is not like that ride. We get one turn, one ticket. Everything is transient.

Three recent events have rammed this truth home.

Speaking of holidays, the first event was a breakaway for a few days. Kay and I went to a holiday spot where we had had many happy family times, but now we were returning as a couple, the children being grown up. The place reverberated with memories. I remembered the giggle of my willowy 12-year-old daughter, now a sophisticated thirty-something. I walked by the communal barbecue grill and paused to stand on the very spot where, two decades ago, my 7-year-old son watched me cremate hamburgers. The place echoes with what used to be and will never be again. I confess that our breakaway was a little spoiled by nostalgia.

Then there were the three days that Kay and I spent clearing my mother's house. Mugged by the evil thug that is dementia, she has been getting progressively worse, sometimes thinking that I'm her son, sometimes that I'm her brother, and alternating between tenderness and anger with a frightening speed. She is now in a wonderful care facility and, for the most part, seems to be enjoying it. Sometimes we phone her and she is too busy with her activities to talk to us, which is strangely wonderful, because we want her to get fully integrated into her new life. Anyway, we went through every wardrobe, and every drawer, most of them stuffed with bills that had been paid a decade or so ago. We found the grimy fingerprints of dementia everywhere. We filled dozens of plastic bags, and I took them to the dump. It was all rubbish, but I felt an irrational shame as, so easily, I discarded her history, tossing her stuff onto a stinking pile. Thumbing through photograph albums, (treasures that we have kept) we looked at the young, hopeful, good-looking couple that was my parents. Nothing lasts.

The third event is a wildfire that is burning in Colorado right now – the most devastating in the history of the state. Over eighty thousand acres have burned, and nearly five hundred homes have been reduced to ash. We are in no current danger, but from our house we can see a huge plume of smoke. The air is thick (and dangerous to those with breathing problems) and, even as I write, I cough occasionally because of the acrid fumes. Everything is covered with a smoky film. Our church service last weekend was built entirely around what is unfolding as a disaster. Again, nothing lasts.

All of this makes me want to learn to live in the now, and in the hope of a Christ-centred tomorrow. I don't want to live a postponed existence. Paul Tournier once said that most people spend their whole lives indefinitely preparing to live, and I don't want to be like most people. I don't want to be permanently craning my neck to try to catch a glimpse of what's hopefully ahead. Nor do I want to constantly look back at the past. I just want to savour every moment, but not cling to it, nor have to have it prised from my grasp. Any advice, Adrian?

And here's the part that I could really use your help with. Often Christians use the phrase, 'living in the light of eternity', which makes perfect sense if you live under constant threat of persecution, as the early Christians did and as many believers around the world currently do. But how do we do our days with an eternal view on things, when life is pleasant, our days are mostly sunny, and even if we can't go round again on the ride, we really want to enjoy it, and even some maddening music, for as long as we can?

With much love,

Jeff

PS: Looking forward to seeing you and Bridget on Wednesday. Sadly we won't able to stay overnight, so we'll see you first thing.

NINETEEN

Dear Jeff,

Wednesday sounds fine, but it's a shame you can't stay over, because we wanted to try out our new communal shower facility. Now that economics are tight it seems a good plan to bathe with our guests. Maybe if you'd known that earlier you would have decided to stay. Sometimes the dog joins in. It's such fun! Lots of naked, soapy love to you both,

Adrian and Bridget xx

TWENTY

Dear Adrian,

Am gutted to miss sudsy fellowship. Sounds like a perfect development now that many churches are getting into 'messy church'. What better follow-on could there be than communal showering? Could also lead to useful small groups (although one would need a larger shower cubicle, and someone willing to get their acoustic guitar a little damp). My only worry . . . the presence of the roving dog. Might not be good.

Jeff

TWENTY-ONE

Hi Jeff,

I resonated with so much that you said about the transience of life. Such a pool of sweet sadness in the things that you wrote about. I remember throwing away my mother's brochure from her incredibly short trip on the Queen Elizabeth from France to England(!), something she had wanted to do for the whole of her financially impoverished existence, and finally managed, in miniature, as it were, when she had a little money towards the end of her active life. It felt like some sort of murderous act throwing that glossy bit of nonsense into the bin, but mum would certainly have laughed at me and told me to get on with it and stop being a silly fool.

I do miss her, Jeff. I don't want her to be dead. A little sob escaped me as I wrote those words. Bridget feels the same about her mum and dad. Stupid, sodding death! I hate it as much as Jesus did. Can you imagine the tear-soaked triumph in his voice as he said those (truly) immortal words, 'Fear not, I have overcome death!'

Mourning the temporary also rings a lot of bells. I remember something I said to Bridget when the children were at an age when we would take them for long walks, come back, throw them in the bath, then sit round the fire

eating a ridiculously large tea while we watched something stupid on television. 'Do you realise, Bridget,' I said
when they were finally in bed after one of these burning
red and gold autumn evenings, 'that we're living in a
time that our children won't even reflect on, until it
becomes the past for each one of them?'

Sometimes I want those days back, but we do have a
very deliberate strategy nowadays. We are keen to amass a
lot of memories for ourselves in this part of our lives. Every
day is a chance to do something that is, at the very least,
enjoyable, and occasionally even memorable. I'm with
Dylan Thomas. I have no intention of going gentle into that
goodnight, albeit for rather different reasons. Some of this is
about being a little kinder to ourselves than we have been,
and some of it is about never giving up the opportunity to
go for projects that really interest us. For instance, the house
we have recently moved into has a barn (yes, a barn!) in the
garden, and it cries out to be converted into a further living
area that we could use to give respite to idiots like us who
rush around madly, and suddenly need a place where
people will be Jesus for them and probably never even
mention his name. It's a project, and I think we'll go for it.

As for 'living in the light of eternity', well, another one
for the blender I think. Phrases like this are really beginning to make my spleen ache, to use a theological expression. Recently a woman in a service I was at told everyone
that God was going to 'inhabit our praise'. Why do we do
this? Why do we, Jeff? Why do we talk about God and the
things of God as though it would be dangerous to communicate in normal English? Yes, I know we're always
banging on about this, but a recent phone call gave me
some ideas on this particular subject.

My old friend John Hall rang me a few weeks ago to
ask an interesting question.

'You know the verse,' he said, 'that's usually translated "The love of money is the root of all evil", somewhere in one of the letters to Timothy, isn't it?'

'Yes,' I said, 'I know the one, but I couldn't have told you where it is.'

'Don't you think that's a bit odd? I mean, how can money be the root of *all* evil? Seems a bit over the top, doesn't it?'

John is a lot cleverer than I am, and I feel quite sure he didn't really need my opinion on the subject, but it was nice of him to ask. Sadly, I had nothing helpful to say at all. After I'd put the phone down I fetched my trusty concordance and looked it up.

Speaking of concordances by the way, Jeff, it was a shock and a revelation to me when I discovered many years ago that sermonisers and preachers were not in possession of the encyclopaedic knowledge of the Bible that I innocently assumed they must be. I would have said that a concordance was probably some kind of musical instrument if anyone had asked me. I was truly amazed at the way in which speakers leaped from scripture to scripture like supercharged gazelles, picking out references to their theme. Nowadays, of course, I am one of that herd and I can cheat with the best of them – or rather, I could if I wanted to.

Anyway, I finally found the verse by looking under 'root', and there it was in 1 Timothy 6. A little more research revealed that some versions state that 'the love of money is a root of all kinds of evil', while most of the others use the more familiar form suggesting that it is the basis of *all* evil. So if, I asked myself, this latter translation is the correct one, what could it possibly mean?

I sat down and googled – not the internet, but my own head. There's a world of interesting things tucked away in the universe of our minds, and even if the mind is relatively feeble, it can produce and provoke some intriguing connections if you don't get too organised about it. One of the first things that occurred to me was something Jesus said about there being three things that will weigh a man's heart down if he is not careful. Back to the jolly old concordance. There it was. Luke 21:34. I was right. Three things. One is dissipation, one is drunkenness and the third is anxieties of life.

Reading this verse again took me down a rather overgrown side-turning in the tangled forest of my memory. It must have been in the mid-eighties that Bridget and I found ourselves enjoying a cup of tea and some worryingly strange cake in the company of Malcolm and Kitty Muggeridge at their home in Sussex. Malcolm had been engaged to join us for some television recordings on the following day, and we had been invited to his home to talk about the content of our broadcasts. By then Muggeridge was advanced in age, and a little confused about practical matters (he had forgotten whether it was radio or television we were doing), but I was childishly excited about meeting him. When Bridget and I were living with John Hall in the Bromley area in the early seventies, we always said that this man would be our first choice as someone to invite to tea. We never did, but here I was more or less fulfilling our dream. So exciting!

As we talked, the subject of alcohol arose. Malcolm, by now converted to Christianity, of course, and heavily into very public repentance, declared that he had spent most of his life wandering around European cities in an alcoholic haze. Keen to sound attentive and knowledgeable, I said something along the lines of, 'Ah yes, it's striking, isn't it, that drunkenness is one of the specific things mentioned by Jesus that can weigh a man's heart down.'

Malcolm fixed me with a gleaming, challenging eye, and said in his customary wide-mouthed, growling voice, 'I think you'll find that Jesus never specifically mentioned drunkenness.'

So in awe was I of my literary hero that I came close to expunging that verse from my memory and agreeing with him. However a little sanity prevailed and I found the reference for him. Afterwards I said to Bridget, 'I corrected Malcolm Muggeridge. Did you notice?'

Leaving all that aside, I guess that this biblical reference to drunkenness can be taken to include any of the addictions or single-issue fanaticisms that men and women are prone to embrace. And the fact is that many of these obsessions can very convincingly suggest quite laudable concerns with spiritual matters. End-times, healing, miracles, praise and worship, tradition, language, styles of churchmanship, funny voices, human optimism; all of these things and many more can be used as substitutes for scary encounters with the God who functions as a genuine, unaffected, relaxed presence in environments where the fake uniforms and brassy bling of churchy rubbish haven't got a chance.

Why is love of money the root of all evil? Because it implies an obsession with the means of obtaining good things instead of actually using those means to collect the good things themselves. Why is the love of that list of things I've just mentioned the root of all evil? Because they are not intended to be the objects of our love. They are supposed to be the means by which we find our way into the presence of this God who might actually exist (!) and be waiting for followers of Jesus to bottom out into being who they are, and truly, honestly, fearfully follow him into bus shelters and palaces and shopping malls and slums and wine-bars and laundrettes and our own kitchens and sitting rooms, with no false armour, and somehow live with feeling so naked that we need him desperately.

In the end, that's my answer to your question, Jeff. Don't live in the light of eternity, not least because we have no idea what it means, but live now, colliding with things and people, enjoying and laughing and weeping and getting angry as Jesus did. And let's keep our fascinated and newly refreshed eyes open to see what he might do through us when we give up Christianity and follow him. Maybe living in the light of eternity actually means that we consistently engage with 'now', because, within the plans of God, future and past will look after themselves.

God bless,
Adrian

TWENTY-TWO

Dear Adrian,

Before I say anything of substance (there's presumption for you) let me congratulate you and Bridget in acquiring a barn. This is incredibly exciting, assuming that what you have got is actually more than an oversized shed, and you're not just getting a little carried away. But in rereading your aspirations for it, it seems that you are planning to convert it (one assumes this does not involve any evangelistic initiatives) into a place where people can actually stay, which would be a bit ambitious if it were little more than a tumbledown cedar construction used to store broken earthenware pots at the end of the garden. I have visions of a lovely place with gnarled timbers and the faint smell of cow poo from former inhabitants that have long since graduated into hamburgers, with you stomping around in a tweed jacket and designer wellies and Bridget popping off to see James Herriot in the Range Rover with the Labradors in the back . . .

. . . sorry, got a bit carried away with the thought of you being officially part of the landed gentry. Anyway, I'm thrilled for you. I hope when it's soundly converted, that you'll repeat the invitation for Kay and I to stay, although I'm glad to affirm that the communal showering you mentioned earlier was said in jest. I hope. We don't own a Labrador, but perhaps could rent one for the weekend.

Thanks for what you said about 'living in the light of eternity' and other religious clichés. I certainly get your point about the verbal mazes that we create with jargon and slogans. And while there's so much about Jesus that I don't begin to understand, I do know he is more than a little irritated when we take what should be a pathway and turn it into a maze that would not look out of place at Hampton Court. He had a damning verdict about the smug religious barons of his day; I love Eugene Petersen's version of Matthew 23:4–7 in *The Message*

> Instead of giving you God's Law as food and drink by which you can banquet on God, they package it in bundles of rules, loading you down like pack animals. They seem to take pleasure in watching you stagger under these loads, and wouldn't think of lifting a finger to help. Their lives are perpetual fashion shows, embroidered prayer shawls one day and flowery prayers the next. They love to sit at the head table at church dinners, basking in the most prominent positions, preening in the radiance of public flattery, receiving honorary degrees, and getting called 'Doctor' and 'Reverend.'[2]

I've found myself lost in a forest of clichés more than once. I mentioned some earlier, but there's more. When I hear 'We're on the edge of a breakthrough in the heavenlies', 'Let go and let God', 'Prayer is a conversation', or I'm asked 'How many sense that the presence of the Lord is here tonight?' (as if the assurance that the Architect of the Universe is among his creation is a matter to vote on, like some kind of cosmic Eurovision Song Contest, with Terry Wogan finally announcing that yes, 64 points, God is actually here), then I want to scream something naughty. I totally agree that prattling endlessly on about these churchy things can be just like the love of money, where we're obsessed with the shadow rather than the substance, and our churchgoing feeds an addiction with the irrelevant.

I fully appreciate how a phrase like 'living in the light of eternity' would therefore make you curl your lip and snort like one of the former inhabitants of your shed, sorry, barn. But at the risk of sounding like I'm disagreeing (but hey, you corrected Malcolm Muggeridge), surely one of the damnable things about clichés is that they repel us away from a truth that is actually vital. You see, there's got to be something about forever that changes the way we live today, and I'm not talking about the mad chart-waving eschatological speculators who bang on endlessly about Israel doing that and Iraq doing this and silly computations with numbers that are supposed to mean something but don't. I'm not talking about the murderous treatment of the book of Revelation, where enthusiastic preachers have taken a poem and turned it into a timetable, or literalised it so that Christians die thinking they are going to stroll around on thirty-two carat pavements. But there does seem to be a lot in Scripture about what's on the horizon, Adrian. The early Christians seemed very focused on it, Paul didn't seem to be able to make up his mind about whether to stick around here or head out for there, and Revelation was apparently a circular letter designed to encourage struggling souls to hang on, because ultimately God wins.

I think the idea of a future reality making a difference to our present reality (there you go, I've tossed 'living in the light of eternity' into the skip) is burrowed deep in my consciousness because of an event which turned what should have been one of the happiest days of my life, into one of the most horrifying.

I was graduating from three years at Bible college, where I didn't learn much (entirely my own fault, I was more interested in table tennis than identifying the author of Hebrews, and was actually found bashing a ping-pong ball around during the Greek exam). Kay had travelled down to witness a ceremony where I, in the presence of other smiling and more accomplished graduates, would be presented with a certificate confirming my lack-lustre results. The sun was shining upon the gentle Surrey hills (the college was just outside Dorking), and we had a guest speaker coming in from what was Rhodesia, now Zimbabwe, to address us.

Early that morning, the telephone jangled in the principal's office, and he took a call that changed his life, and ours with it. Our missionary speaker had boarded the plane in Rhodesia, leaving behind thirteen missionary colleagues. A band of terrorists had crossed the Mozambique border, raided the mission station, raped the women, and slaughtered them all. The terrible news swept around the college like a tsunami wave.

A student was despatched to wait at the college gates for our speaker to arrive – he had no idea that all his dear friends and colleagues were dead. He was ushered into the principal's office, told the devastating news, whereupon he decided that, even in his trauma and grief, he still needed to address the student body. I don't remember the details of the sermon, but I'll never forget the heart of it, because he spoke on Paul's words 'For me to live is Christ, to die is gain.'

Later we heard that one of the female missionaries, standing in a bloody, screaming line, waiting to die, called out, 'Don't worry, Phil, they can't kill the soul!' When the crunch came, eternity really did matter. Perhaps I'm partially answering my own question, Adrian: when you're facing the last moments, or living with the constant threat of persecution as Paul and his friends did (and as members of the persecuted church around the world do now), then eternity does loom very large. It has to. In the meantime, in the comfort and ease of what we're currently living (although I am suffering from an irrational dose of barn envy), perhaps what we need to do, as you say, is be totally and utterly present in the now. Surely there's nothing wafty or ethereal about genuinely having a strong hope for forever.

Before I close, allow me to return to the delicious thought of that barn of yours, Squire Adrian, and your plan to make it a place where harassed souls can come to stay for a while. It prompted a memory of some of the hellish accommodation arrangements that I've endured as a Christian speaker over the years. Next time I write, I'll tell you a little more (if you're interested, so let me know), but suffice it to say that I've stayed in a brothel, an unfinished basement, and in a Bates-type motel where a masked man knocked on my door and threatened my life if I presumed to flush the toilet. I'd love to hear of some of the exotic places where you have proverbially hung your hat. Lords of the manor do wear hats, don't they?

With love,

Jeff

TWENTY-THREE

Hi Jeff,

Thanks for your response to my comments about living in the thingummy of whatsit. I suppose one of the things that fuels and excites me about the mystery of Jesus stuff, is the way in which we have to continually negotiate chewy paradoxes and somehow incorporate these awkwardly shaped items into the daily business of real life. G.K. Chesterton was an expert in this field. I recall him saying (when I had tea with him once) that 'if you stretch monotony far enough it will break with a sound like a song.' Happily married people will certainly know what this means. Chesterton's paradoxes are almost always signposts to a truth that we own but have never fully excavated from the depths of ourselves. The paradox illustrated by Jesus in his clear intention to live fully and vigorously in tiny moments (drawing his energy and inspiration from an awareness of the bigger picture as well as an unbelievably massive backdrop of divine intention), can potentially put fuel in anyone's tank, once they understand what it means.

As I was writing these words I remembered a moment when I was in Tunbridge Wells the other day. I was sitting outside a café in the sun having a black coffee and a cheese scone spread with far too much butter (Come on, Kendrick – get to the real stuff!). At the table next to me two fairly elderly women were getting ready to leave. It was a bit breezy, and one of the ladies patted her hair and said to the other one, 'Does my hair look all right? I had it done on Friday, but it's a bit blowy this morning.' Her friend reassured her.

They were a funny old couple, and I don't suppose anyone was likely to notice the state of their hair, or anything else about the way they looked, for that matter. But they cared. I shed a little tear. Probably because that attitude reminded me a little bit of both my mother and Bridget's. The tiny things remained important however old they became, and however the broad context of their lives might have seemed to militate against trivia. They were two of the kindest, most generous people I have known, and they could have taught you and I a great deal about how to live and love and enjoy, as though human life and eternity were two streets in the same neighbourhood.

That was a terrible, wonderful story about the missionaries who were murdered. The same thing applies, though. Crying out encouragement to others at a time when you are facing imminent horrific death yourself, is a street in this world, meeting and providing a well-paved path to a street in the next. These Gethsemanes are tortuous, glorious places.

We saw something similar in Zambia in 2004 when, as World Vision representatives, we were learning about AIDS work that was being carried out by World Vision workers. Proper treatment and care were scarce in the villages, and most available Christian teaching centred on hope for the future, the possibility of peace and reunion in heaven. Always, though, the major concern for women with no husbands or older relatives was their children. I think some of the brave women we met would have given up their eternal hope like a shot if it had meant that their children would be properly cared for after their death. Living in the light of eternity offers very little satisfaction when you know that your children will be starving in the darkness of this world.

I must say, by the way, on a very much lighter note, that I was intrigued and profoundly amused by your explanation of why you didn't learn much at Bible college. My goodness, Jeff, you really did live a life of sin and debauchery at that college, didn't you? When others were studying Greek and working hard to absorb abstruse theological principles, what was the young Jeff Lucas doing? Was he smoking weed and injecting heroin and having to be dragged home every night in an alcoholic stupor? No, he was not. Was he cruising the streets hunting voraciously for vulnerable women on whom he could slake his filthy lust? No, he was not. Was he allowing himself to be drawn into devil-worshipping covens of snarling God-haters? No, he was not. What was he doing, then?

He was playing ping-pong. Yes, table tennis was his vile drug of choice, and those of us who have never been tempted in this way can only mistily imagine those dark moments of shameful defeat when, with pallid cheeks and crazed, feverish eyes, he finally threw his Greek lexicon from him, and allowed his clutching hand to wrap itself yet again around the lusciously seductive handle of a favourite ping-pong paddle. There was no going back once that pimpled rubber came into contact with his skin. He was lost. Satan had won. And, lest we forget, ping-pong cannot be played alone. One asks oneself how many other innocent souls were seduced by his moaning, dribbling entreaties into laying aside their proper responsibilities and plunging into a vice that is, God knows, far easier to start than to finish.

I hardly dare to voice a question that should only really be tackled after weeks of deep and constructive counselling, but I'll ask it anyway. Were there sometimes – doubles?

Honestly, you were a lad and no mistake, Jeff. I once played pick-a-stick for Smarties, but a good friend saw what was happening and took me away to his house in the country for a week. I went cold turkey and came back clean.

Speaking of houses in the country, your subtle mockery of our barn is quite misplaced. It's much more than an oversized shed, there's no smell of cow poo, and I sincerely hope that Bridget won't be going off to see James Herriot, as that would involve an exhumation and she's as likely to take up ping-pong as get into body-snatching. No, it's a really substantial stone building on two floors with all the plumbing and electrical connections you'd need for a separate dwelling area. Could be very exciting. Come and stay as soon as you can, and we'll drive up to Durham Cathedral for evensong, one of my favourite experiences in the world.

Hellish accommodation during our travels? Well, I don't think I've experienced anything quite as dramatic as you, but some have definitely been interesting. I remember we once stayed in a bed and breakfast establishment where we had been offered an en-suite bedroom. Our room, opening off the kitchen for some obscure reason, turned out to be what I can only describe as a crevice in the wall, containing the thinnest bed I have ever seen. I suppose two super models might have fitted into it, albeit rather cosily, but Bridget and I would have needed to lie on our sides on top of each other, if you can

– or are willing to – imagine that. One of our first tasks was to explore our 'slot' and discover the en-suite bathroom that we had been assured was part of the deal. Knowing how ingenious designers and planners are nowadays, we spent some time tapping walls and gingerly pushing at things to see if some fiendishly clever, Inca-like construction might be revealed. It was not, and we emerged from our claustrophobic nightmare to be told by our landlady that the 'en-suite' bathroom was across the kitchen, just next to the place where people had breakfast. We did ask, in mildly curious tones, if she could tell us in what sense this could be described as 'en-suite'.

'You're the only people using it,' she said, 'and there's dressing gowns for when you come through the kitchen in front of people in the morning.'

'Oh,' we said.

We didn't sleep much that night. And, as you can imagine, we got up well before breakfast. There are many more memories, but I want to hear about some of yours.

Before I go, I just wanted to tell you about something weird that happened the other day. I can tell you about it because I think you'll understand. Bridget and I got a letter in the post from someone we know. It was the kind of letter you might dream about if you were feeling low and inadequate and useless. Our friend talked to us and about us in such richly glowing terms that I almost blushed as I read it. I didn't know where to put myself. If the contents of that letter had been true, we would have needed to entirely revise the old 'saved by grace' mechanism, because, in our case at least, it simply wouldn't be required.

Like Tony Hancock of old, we would be able to waltz up to the gates of heaven, offer St Peter a sheet of A4 with a list of our qualifications and virtues written on it, and say, 'Add that lot up, mate, and swing those gates wide. We've earned a place in Paradise and we're coming in to claim it!'

At first I was thrilled by that letter, but as the day wore on I felt more and more depressed. I simply was not the person described in that letter. I just wasn't. A dark cloud seemed to descend. By the evening I was feeling rueful but okay. For years I've paid lip-service to the idea that the Holy Spirit in us can perform much more effectively than we are able to in human terms. Truly accepting this is much more difficult. To put it in horribly simplistic terms, I was a bit jealous of God actually being able to do the business. Ring any bells? I'd be interested to know.

Lots of love,
Adrian

TWENTY-FOUR

Dear Adrian,

Thanks for yours, which did cause me to salivate a little, when you mentioned cheese scones with too much butter. I think you're right, we should have worship songs that express gratitude for luscious moments like these. 'Butter' is a tough word for the lyricists, though finding words that rhyme with it is difficult. 'Utter', 'mutter', 'stutter' and indeed 'udder' are not likely candidates.

I wish I could have met the two mothers who were so obviously lovely, Adrian. You and Bridget were rich in having both of them, but that must make the fact that they're not with you now all the more painful.

Those two ladies in the cafe made me think about what it means to be alive, with all that checking of hair that no one notices. Most of that preening is done for our own sakes, and when we stop caring about the little things, we've probably stopped being interested in living. It comes as quite a shock to realise that, young or old, not many people actually notice much about us, especially as we live in a time when people 'do' lunch together, and then sit and stare at their smart phones, texting someone else.

I can totally identify with your day with the clouds gathering. It's ironic, isn't it? We're encouraged because someone sees something of Jesus in us, and then fed up because they don't seem to be aware of all the rubbish which we're all too aware of.

I get weary of the interminable process of being a Christian. Like a child stuck in the back of a hot car in an M25 snarl-up, I want to yell, 'Are we nearly there yet?' but then feel the frustration that we're never really able to begin to answer the wretched question. If we conclude that we're anywhere near arrival, then we're proud. And if we decide we're a million miles off track with a busted GPS, then we're slackers who need to get with the programme. It is infuriating.

You mentioned sometimes feeling jealous of God, I presume, because of the sense that he has arrived. But has he? While I'm not trying to suggest that God is gradually morphing into being what he isn't now, surely he is constantly moved, impacted, and responding? Maybe that means that he is morphing into what he isn't now! (Hold on, I hear the sound of a crackling bonfire. Certainly I don't believe one of the doctrines that I learned when I was not indulging my flesh in the foetid pool of ping-pong: impassibility. It's the idea that God is not moved by what happens to us. He is divinely impervious, and to suggest that he can be affected by us implies some kind of weakness. I think it's utter tosh. Not just for emotional reasons, or that I'd like to make God look like I'd like him to look, but because it seems utterly incongruous with Scripture. There's a reason for our calling the Easter event the Passion.

I was so glad to get my nasty little table tennis secret out into the open. For years I've sat through Christian meetings, wondering what people would think of me if

they knew the truth about my grubby little habit.
Certainly I would have been devastated by an encouraging, blush-inducing letter, Adrian, painfully aware that
the writer did not know my passion for netting and green
tables.

I mentioned that I have stayed in some 'interesting
places' over the years of travelling to pursue this strange
life that is generically described as ministry. Before I say
anything further, I need to offer the required disclaimer
that hopefully will satisfy any reader who might take
offence, thinking that I'm complaining about my life,
while some souls live and serve Jesus in harrowing con-
ditions. Not only do I fully respect those committed disciples, I also fear them. Their wonderful example makes
me feel I'm not actually a Christian. You and I both know
that we are incredibly privileged, and so what follows
here isn't a wail or a rant, but simply me sharing some of
the more challenging moments as I've navigated Planet
Christian.

Notice I've used the words, 'interesting' and 'challenging'. As you know, these are actually code words in
the church. Christians often use 'interesting' when in conversation with someone who is saying something utterly
inane, or sharing a picture that they have had of a rabbit
called Sid with giant paws, representing God's open arms
to the nations. Rather than say something as bold as 'Just
how long have you been tottering on the brink of insan-
ity?' we smile, nod encouragingly, and say, 'Yes, interesting.' And then 'challenging' describes another Christian
whom we'd dearly like to kill. Anyway, back to the
diverse and challenging places that I've stayed in.

First, to the brothel (I never thought I'd ever write that
sentence). I was speaking in a church in Washington,
where the minister was keen to reach his community. He

obviously had very little actual knowledge of it, as he put his guest speaker in a dubious-looking place that served as an activity centre for the local ladies of the night (actually, ladies of the day and night, as it turned out).

All seemed fine when I checked in. I wasn't greeted by a bosomy madam, fag on lip, who asked me if I required any extras (if she had, I would have probably asked if porridge was available in the morning). No, it was the sounds emanating from the rooms around me that worried me. I noticed people were checking in and then checking out after minutes or an hour or two. (One chap checked out after three hours; I didn't know whether to be impressed or appalled.) I finally fled not only because the place felt so seedy but I wasn't sure sleep would be possible. And without sounding like disgusted of Basingstoke, I felt I could taste the despair in the place, where women (and one or two men) were forced to hawk themselves to grubby strangers in order to guarantee the next meal. Forget the lovely Julia Roberts in *Pretty Woman*, which coated prostitution with an undeserved sheen of glamour. This was grimy, inhuman, and soulless.

Then there was the time when I stayed in a basement, or to be more precise, an unfinished cellar, with cold, rough brick walls and a concrete floor. I was speaking at a church where they accommodated guests with members of the congregation rather than in a hotel. This can be nice, assuming that the congregational member is not a serial killer, or the grand master of the local chapter of the Ku Klux Klan.

I think the chap I was staying with was possibly both. He had a home in the middle of nowhere, and wore the hungry look of a long term single man, desperate to find a bride who also loved going into the woods to kill things. Upstairs was relatively comfortable if somewhat rustic, cluttered with the heads of dead animals on the walls, and sporting a gigantic flat screen television. But I was consigned to the unfinished basement, parked on a rickety camp bed jammed between a refrigerator and a chest freezer, which gave rise to unhelpful imaginings as it grew darker. Perhaps the bodies of previous speakers were crammed into the freezer, readily available snacks for when the deer season was over . . .

It was then that I realised that there was a plot, and I was in the middle of it. This strange, confused man was obviously a source of concern in his church, and so the minister had placed me there in order that I might help to sort him out. Over the years this has often happened, Adrian. I have met some truly epic, wonderful souls in my travels – but I've also found myself not so much accommodated in a home, as in an impossible counselling situation. I don't think I was much help to the outdoorsy chap with his basement of fearsome shadows. I kept waking in the night, wondering when he was going to rev up his chain saw.

But my most terrifying incident happened in the bleak midwinter (shall we pause to share a carol?) in Oregon. I was alone, it was snowing hard, and I was booked into a very remote motel. I'm not saying that it was the place that inspired Hitchcock's *Psycho*, but the chap at reception did talk about his mother quite a lot. But when he handed me my room key, he spoke words that should have been accompanied by creepy backing music from the New York Symphony Orchestra: 'I'm putting you in our unit which is at the back of our land, by the river. It's very quiet, very peaceful. The only thing is, we've got just one other guest staying back there, and he's just a little strange, if you get my drift.'

I did not get his drift, and I wanted to get out of there, but it was getting dark, and the snow was falling in great cotton wool blobs, making it difficult for me to drive around to find a hotel without a resident strange person. I drove back to the river unit, which was shrouded in the shadows of some very large trees. A double-storied block, there was just one light on, in an upstairs unit. I was in a ground floor room. I lugged my cases, and my heavier heart, into the frigid room, overwhelmed that I was going to be parked there, away from Kay and our young family, for the next four nights.

Using the bathroom, and following the usual habit of flushing the toilet after use, I was alarmed to hear the stomp, stomp of heavy footsteps from the first floor landing above. I froze. I could hear those footsteps slowly coming down the metal stairs, and now crunching through the snow towards my room. Can you hear the orchestra in the background, Adrian?

It was terrifying. There was silence, and for a few moments I thought he'd gone, perhaps for a walk by the river. Then there were three heavy thuds as he pounded on my door. I looked through the spy hole, and literally jumped back with shock. He was wearing a balaclava, and only a circle of face was visible. But his was the palest skin I have ever seen. Perhaps he had been in a fire, and wore the balaclava to disguise burns on his head. His impossibly whitened face stood out against the dark wool.

I can't believe what I did next, Adrian. I had been warned that the man was strange, it was dark now, and we were alone. But I'm British. I opened the door.

'Yes?' I asked, as if it were perfectly normal to greet a man dressed like a wannabe bank robber who had stopped by for a chat during a snowstorm.

'Are you a preacher?' he grunted. My mind raced. How did he know who I was, and what I did? Was this some kind of Gadarene discernment? Then I realised that the man with the dead mother at reception had probably told him about the other guest that was coming in: a preacher.

Now my mind rushed further, as we stood there in a moment of awkward silence. Was he going to ask for spiritual help? Was he in need of prayerful advice?

'I heard you flush the toilet, preacher. It disturbed me. Don't flush the toilet, okay?'

I was about to protest that, with a four day stay ahead, this might be a challenge, but thought better of it. He stomped off, back to his room.

Challenging. So challenging that I grabbed my bags, jumped in the car, and fled the place. There are no lasting scars from the experience, apart from a momentary pang of guilt when I'm about to flush. The moral of this story? There is none. It has no merit as a potential parable. I just wanted to share some episodes from my journey with you.

I'm glad that you and Bridget managed to survive the night in the crevice with an en-suite. Have you thought of taking up pot-holing?

With love,
Jeff

PS: By the way, thanks for sharing your confusion about what a concordance is, and that you used to think it was some kind of musical instrument. This came as a great relief. Years ago, someone offered to buy me a concordance, and I thought that I too would have to play scales on it while wearing leather shorts and a hat with a large feather in it. Little did I know that a concordance was actually a resource designed to make preachers look cleverer than they are, especially around people who are especially interesting and challenging.

PPS: By the way, just pondering the thought of being jealous of God: if you were God, how would you do things differently?

TWENTY-FIVE

Hi Jeff,

Oh, Jeff, you do make me laugh sometimes. How could all these things happen to one poor preacher? Or is it just that you (and perhaps I also to an extent) have our eyes open to events in a different way?

As for your final question! Ah, how *would* I do things differently if I was God?

Look, are you trying to make me feel guilty? You know what we recovering evangelicals are like. We shout and scream about the way we were made to feel bad about ourselves, and then when a chance for some real old homespun, gloopy guilt appears we grab at it with both hands, just to enjoy a sweet dose of nostalgia about the good old, bad old days. Okay, you asked for it. This is what I would do differently, and he (God that is) can like it or lump it.

First of all, he could heal my sciatica. Not too difficult when you're all-powerful. A friend of mine e-mailed the other day to say that his knee and his hips are completely healed after a meeting he attended somewhere or other. I was genuinely pleased for him, but a part of me was downright jealous.

'Excuse me,' I said to the Creator of the universe, 'but what does someone have to do to get a bit of miraculous attention round here? I need to be fit to do the things you seem to want me to do, so what's the problem? Am I fifth in the queue? Or tenth? Or twenty-fifth? Or three thousand, five hundred and fiftieth? Or what? It's all right for you. You're perfect. Well, I'm not. I want what my friend got, and I want it now.

'If it comes to that,' I continued, warming to my theme, 'how about you just turning up more? Do you hear what I'm saying? I spend a great bunch of my time trying to explain to people why you don't step up to the plate and do your business at a time when they need you most. Well, why don't you? I'm running out of reasons, and the ones I used to use are starting to sound very thin and unconvincing.

'"It's all a mystery." That's one of 'em. "We have to live in the mystery." Why? Why do we have to live in the mystery? Only because you won't solve it! Why can't we live in the solution? We don't want a load of men in bad beards standing around rocking on their heels and looking intense, we want a bit of action. Look, all you have to do is concentrate. Focus on individual needs. Make it happen, then they'll go and tell everyone else and the people they tell will believe in you, won't they? See what I mean? Surely you want that, don't you? Excuse me, are you listening? Have you heard a single word I've said?'

Seriously, Jeff, there are times when I just want to shake God. And I'll tell you about one of those times. Only a few weeks ago, this youngish man whom I shall call Bob came to see me and said he wanted to ask my advice. My very soul wrinkles like a prune when people say that sort of thing, but it's sort of my job, and anyway, I'm far too interested in people to refuse. So, along he came, and for a long time we sat in silence and he didn't seem able to say what was on his mind, just sat there fiddling with a loose thread in the fabric of the arm of his chair. That's not unusual, so I waited and tried to look as open, and unshockable and compassionate as I could. Finally he spoke.

'I want to be a pastoral worker,' he said.

'Right.'

'But I don't see how I can be one.'

Pause.

'Right.'

'You see, I want to really help people and introduce them to Jesus and tell them he loves them.'

'That sounds good.'

'Yes, but I can't because I don't know if he does.'

'You can't introduce people to Jesus and tell them he loves them, even though you want to, because you don't know if he does. Is that right?'

Silence.

'Do you mean you don't know if he loves you in particular, or the people you might try to help, or just anybody?'

'Well, not me, so – perhaps not anybody.'

Long silence.

'It was my Christian youth leader. He did things to me when I was young.'

'What did he do?'

The young man abruptly snatched his face away to one side as though he had been slapped. His voice when he replied was that of a whimpering child.

'Don't want to say . . .'

'You don't have to.'

Silence.

'Bad things.'

'Right.'

'I asked God over and over again to stop it, but he didn't. I used to cry at night and beg God to make it not happen any more. He didn't do what I asked. He could have done, but he didn't.'

Bob went on to tell me about the things that had been suggested to him in the years following by people who had clearly been genuinely anxious to help heal this pain from the past. One minister had explained that, one day, when he arrived in heaven, Bob would understand. It hadn't helped. Another person had encouraged Bob to look back at the awful situations he had been in, and picture Jesus there with him.

'Did that help?'

'No. If he was there, why didn't he help? Why didn't he stop it?'

'Has anything helped?'

'Not really.'

'But despite all that's happened – and not happened – something in you still wants to feel loved by Jesus and to pass that love on to others.'

'Yes. Don't know why.'

We sat in silence for quite a long time after that. I long ago gave up saying things for the sake of filling silences, and in any case, I had no idea what to suggest. Basically, I could see Bob's point perfectly clearly. Why hadn't God turned up when he was needed? Eventually, Jeff, something did occur to me, and it was something that this young man had never considered, and might well help him. I'll tell you what it was in my next letter, but in the meantime, what do you think? What would you have said? I really want to know.

Yours,

Adrian

TWENTY-SIX

Dear Adrian,

Let me respond to your question about the young man who was abused by his youth leader, and say that my fear would be that I would jump in and say something useless. At least I don't think I would repeat what the others said: I wouldn't say that when he gets to heaven he will understand, because that implies that everything happens for a reason, which is a great idea but doesn't work. And why suggest that he pictures Jesus being with him? Wouldn't that make it worse, if he was present but not doing anything?

I could blather on about the nature of the universe, and the reality that we don't live in a puppet theatre where God is pulling the strings, jerking our collars whenever we do something minor wrong – like playing ping-pong when one should be sitting an examination – or awful, like robbing a young person of their innocence. I could say God certainly doesn't always get his way, and perhaps I'd want to do that, because some Christians seem to take the *if it happened, it was meant to be* approach to life, insisting that because of something called the sovereignty of God, everything that happens is his will. It can't be true, because we wouldn't be told to pray 'your kingdom come, your will be done' if it automatically is. Besides, God is not totally sovereign over me, even though, most or some of the time, I want him to be.

I could launch into a seminar about the nature of the earth and spiritual warfare and bad forces versus good and ultimate justice and God being a Redeemer, so that although he's not the architect of such abuse, he can bring something good out of it. And all that, blah, blah, blah.

I believe all of the above, Adrian. But I think that I'd probably have to come back to the notion of you wanting to shake God, because despite all that is true about the nature of the world we live in, I'd still be angry at what looks pretty much like merciless abandonment to me. And so I'd tell that young man that it is all right to have a rant at God, because Jesus did. I touched on this earlier, but it's relevant here: left alone on the bloody cross, Jesus felt that stony silence, that total loneliness that every human feels sometimes, and yelled out 'My God, my God, why have you forsaken me?' I think it's okay to be wildly irrational before God, and tell him that we'd like it if he'd kill abusers with a swift lightning bolt, but of course be gracious to us when we mess up our own lives, or the lives of others.

I'd tell him that I was really, really sorry, that he was treated so horribly in a place where he should have felt safe. And I suppose I'd like to say that somehow, he is something of a miracle, because he still feels the need to let people know that God loves them, and that, as someone who had decided to try to live in the face of abandonment, he was especially qualified.

But what I want to know is this, Adrian. What on earth did you say?

God bless,
Jeff

TWENTY-SEVEN

Hello Jeff,

Thanks for your frank answer to my query. Isn't it odd when someone asks you such a direct question without saying what they think, and you're left to write stuff that sounds sort of all right, but might be regarded as trite or impotent by the other person? Fortunately, you are never trite, Jeff, and I know you are always searching around for ideas and ploys that actually help people, as opposed to trotting out half-baked propositions that make you feel better but leave your victim exactly where he was in the first place.

I agree with much of what you said, especially the notion that Bob is a bit of a living miracle, given his desire to pass on the love of a God who seemed to fail him so badly when his need was greatest. How do we help those who, in their heart of hearts, feel that, because of blatant neglect, they have been abused, not only by a human being, but by God as well? Maybe this is why Bob goes on yearning for the fulfilment of a dream that turned so grotesquely into a nightmare. He just wants his Daddy. Perhaps Daddy was away on business and simply couldn't be there at the time. Perhaps Daddy's in prison, accused of something he didn't do, and there will come a day when Bob will walk onto the platform of a little country railway station, and a train will come in, and Daddy will step down onto the platform and stand with his arms outstretched, waiting to gather Bob up and say, 'I'm so very sorry – I do love you as much as you ever hoped that I did, and now I'm here to prove it to you.' Perhaps, perhaps, perhaps.

I know a woman who lives on one solitary word of warmth spoken by her human father on his deathbed. Many Christians are yearning for the same experience with their heavenly Father. One word. One arrow of love to break and heal their hearts. So many books, so many sermons, so much theology, such an aching void in the place where something really needs to happen.

What did I say to Bob?

Of course, I have to come clean here. I may be willing and able to agree and rant wildly on behalf of those who are angered or deeply saddened by God, but there is a chamber in my heart that is delightfully filled and furnished with the humour and the love and the sorrow and the tears and the sheer playfulness of God. His ways are weird, and his choices are inexplicable, but – you know what, Jeff? I trust him. I trust, not without pain, in him, and to a lesser extent in me, that in some way that is fully logical in divine terms, he is totally in charge of the whole Bob situation.

That's not what I said to Bob. What did I say to Bob? Well, in one sense it was nothing new, but for him it was an opportunity to wrench his thinking round into a different direction and find a way (almost as narrow as that 'en-suite' bathroom I mentioned) to walk with greater confidence into his own future.

First of all I asked Bob if he had ever watched *Open All Hours*, the situation comedy starring Ronnie Barker as a tight-fisted shopkeeper who hated to close because it might mean losing some extra smidgeon of income.

'Yes,' he said, 'I have seen that. Why?'

'The thing is that God is on duty and behind the counter even more tirelessly than Arkwright. In fact, he never closes. So, here's my question for you. Do you want to join him behind the counter and lend a hand, or do you want to be a grumbling customer for the rest of your life?'

Silence.

'I think I want to help, but . . .'

Bob's 'but' hung in the air between us for several seconds. I helped him out.

'But what about the stuff that happened to you when you were young, and the fact that God let you down? What about that?'

'Well, yes, what about that?'

'Bob, I'm going to do something I don't generally do when people ask me for advice. I'm going to read you a bit from the Bible. And a very odd bit it is.'

I picked up the Gideon Bible I recently stole from the place where I work and read a chunk from the first chapter of Paul's letter to the Colossians. I've copied it out here for you.

> Now I rejoice in what was suffered for you, and I fill up in my flesh what is still lacking in regard to Christ's afflictions, for the sake of his body, which is the church.

'Either I'm going mad,' I said to Bob, 'which is entirely possible, or Paul is saying here that his own suffering is needed to top up the pain that Jesus went through on the cross, so that, in some impossible to understand way, it can be transfigured and used to help the people who need it, the customers who fill the boss's shop twenty-four hours a day. Or to put it another way, Bob, excrement is manure – or it can be after it's been donated.'

'So what you're saying is . . .'

I waited for Bob to finish but he didn't.

'I'm not saying. That's not important. Do you want to know what I believe God is saying?'

Deep sigh.

'All right.'

I dipped into my little chamber for a spot of refreshment and inspiration.

'I believe God is saying this: "Bob, I want to do two things. I want to tell you how I feel about what happened to you, and I want to ask you a favour. First of all, I want you to know that my heart is broken by what happened to you. It cannot be changed or removed or rationalised or redefined and I don't want it to be. It was terrible and yes, I could have stopped it but I didn't. I'm going to shock you by saying that I'm glad I didn't stop it. If I needed tissues you would have to hand me one now. It is utterly impossible for me to explain that statement to you in a form that will make any sense at all to you in this place and at this time. Why should you accept that? You shouldn't. I wouldn't."'

'"But that brings me to the favour I want to ask. Bob, would you be kind enough to help me, not just despite the things that happened in the past. You need to fully acknowledge all that darkness and pain. Grip it. Own it. It is yours to do with as you wish. And here's the biggest favour of all. Please would you be generous enough to give me that pain? Let me nail it up on the cross of my Son and use it for the help and salvation of many, many people. I promise you it didn't happen for that reason, but it would be terrible to waste it now. As for love. Can you bring yourself to trust me just enough to come round behind the counter and find out how we do things? I will teach you how much I love you, and how to offer my love to others but for now you will have to take my hand and follow hopefully. My beloved Son once said, 'My sorrow is so great that it almost crushes me.' It didn't quite crush him, though. He drank his cup of suffering to the last drop, and the world changed. Come and lend us a hand, Bob. We need you. We are open all hours.'''

That's more or less what I said, Jeff, and of course, it's horses for courses and all that. But it did seem to open a few windows that Bob never realised he had access to.

By the way, your account of your friend's suffering at the hands of her father reminded me of a dark moment when I sat with a friend who never talked much about his childhood. I asked him what his dad had been like. He became very still, and his eyes retreated into some inner night.

'He was a minister,' he said at last, 'very much respected. He was a prick when he went to bed at night, and he was a prick when he got up in the morning.'

Maybe you and I use humour so much because it's one of the few ways to cope with all this darkness. Tell me something funny, Jeff. Make me and God laugh, there's a good chap.

> Love as always,
> Adrian

TWENTY-EIGHT

Dear Adrian,

Well, here's an odd thing: your response to Bob is pretty much what I would have expected of you, and yet I confess that I had absolutely no idea what you were going to actually say. Perhaps that's worth explaining, and I'll begin by asking if you've ever been to the Planetarium in London?

I went there three hundred years ago on a school trip, initially under protest. I was far keener to skip to the other attraction that sits next door to the large domed edifice in Baker Street, Madame Tussauds. Not terribly interested to know how far Jupiter was from Uranus. I wanted to cancel our one hour perusal of the heavens above and get right to the waxwork figures of the Beatles, the Queen, and especially Crippen, the poisoner and his gaggle of creepy pals that were waiting to worry us in the Chamber of Horrors. As it turns out, the Planetarium proved to be rather interesting, with its projector that's as big as a detached house, but I mention it because that's where I think most Christians head to when they meet someone like your friend Bob.

In short, we flip into cosmic mode. We crack open our theological charts and pontificate about the mechanics of meaning and desperately try to break some hidden code that will help us make sense of all the vile happenings that daily occur on this beautiful, broken planet of ours. And trips to the Planetarium have their place, because Bob's story (or something as equally painful) is being endlessly repeated every second of every day around this wretched, busted earth.

To switch the analogy for a moment, sometimes I feel that when I have to fly somewhere. It's late at night, the plane drops down to about ten thousand feet, and I look out over the sparkling lights of a city; roads, houses and cars stretch out like an illuminated toy town for as far as the eye can see. I'm always tempted in that moment to think that I'm looking at something beautiful, Adrian, to romanticise the scene. But then I look again, and realise that down there, in the brightly lit vista, women are being raped, children ignored or worse, spiteful words are being hurled into the faces of the timid, schemes to hurt are being hatched. Of course, down there among the streetlights, scenes of beauty are playing out, with happy marriages, loving families and good things. Down there is laughter and love too.

But it's all so mixed up, isn't it, and as the captain tells us to put our seats belts on and we drop down another five hundred feet, banking for the final approach, I wonder then what it feels like to be God, to see it all, to hear it all, to be a witness to everything. That's when I want some kind of concrete explanation. I want the narrator in the Planetarium to tell me exactly how a black hole works, and what's stopping our plane from being squashed by a passing meteorite, what those rings around Saturn are for, and why that leering monster is doing something so unspeakable to a terrified child.

You didn't rush to the Planetarium with Bob, and force him to sit up, crane his neck, and listen to a lecture.

Somehow I knew you wouldn't, which is one of the many reasons that I'm glad you're alive. No, instead of looking out there somewhere, you looked closely at him, heard his cry and didn't try to fit everything together neatly. You brought brown-coated Barker into the room, and introduced Bob to *Open All Hours* Arkwright. And in talking about the shattered heart that God has for Bob and his terrible pain, and then Paul 'topping up' Jesus' sufferings, you gently challenged Bob to make a choice between being a tetchy customer, or a helper behind the counter. Instead of reaching for the stars, you really did reach out to Bob. What you said and did was risky, Adrian. You said you trust God, and I believe you, because *Exhibit A* in demonstrating that trust was the way that you spoke to Bob, suggesting that you were actually speaking on God's behalf. But I think you were able to do that, because you listened to, thought about, prayed for, and actually saw . . . Bob.

Isn't that what we all want, Adrian? To be noticed? Isn't that why old ladies, whom, as you rightly say, few notice, check that their hair is looking nice? Isn't that why small children say 'Look, Daddy' when they ride their wobbly bikes for twenty yards? It's because we know that, much of the time, we're met with glazed-eyed indifference fuelled by lives lived at terminal velocity, and we'd just love the luxury of someone seeing us for a little while. It begins at birth with a cry for attention and ends with us hoping that a few people will show up at our funerals. Not just for the free cheese sandwiches, but that they'll notice that we were there, and have gone. Of course, the attendance figures of our funerals will make no difference to us whatsoever, but we die hoping that our passing will be acknowledged.

You noticed Bob. What you didn't do was quantify him, file him under a heading, or gaze with mild, clinical interest at him, and then hurry on, as I did when I passed through the tableaux of obscure European royal families in Tussauds.

And you didn't try to minimise his pain.

That leads me to share a little liturgy with you. I don't know much about how liturgy works, although I have come to love the few liturgical experiences that I have had. Much of the time, especially when I'm pondering pain at fifteen thousand feet, I'm speechless, so the words of others are helpful; I told you earlier about my experience with the wonderful Anglo-Catholic group. I love the simple sharing of the peace, and have modelled a very basic piece of liturgy around the idea of a two sentence exchange: 'The Lord be with you.' 'And also with you.' An idea, a blessing, a response.

Every year, my Mum and I have shared a Christmas liturgy; just the two of us. In fact, it's so intimate, I've wondered about sharing it, but here goes. It may be that her dementia is going to rob us of even this tradition. Each year, a few days before Christmas Day, we go to visit the grave of her parents. My grandmother was a smiling, gorgeous soul; I never once heard her say anything remotely spiteful. But she had the misfortune to be married to my grandfather, a vicious, spiteful bully, a booze-fuelled thug who verbally, and sometimes physically, battered his family into submission.

At eighty five, my mother still bears the emotional scars of his abuse. And so we go to the grave, and my mum carries just one Christmas wreath, always a wreath for her mother, and, pointedly, no wreath for her father. And we stand there, and she cries, and remembers, and then she always asks me to say a prayer. It's then, Adrian, before I pray, that we share the liturgy. It goes like this:

Me: Mum, he was a bastard, wasn't he?

Mum: (Crying): Yes, he really was.

Just like your friend who was cursed to have a 'much respected' ministerial father, who was also a perennial prick, so it's important for my mum to be able to know that her pain isn't ignored or forgotten, but seen.

You asked me to make you laugh, Adrian. And I will try, honest. But for now, thanks for seeing Bob, and introducing him to Arkwright, and Jesus.

With love as ever,

Jeff

TWENTY-NINE

Dear Jeff,

I did go to the Planetarium when I was quite small, and I found it quite awesome, not least because I simply could not work out what was going on. Had I somehow, magically, been transported into outer space, or had they taken the roof off this vast building and accelerated the passing of time so that we were able to witness the night sky at eleven o'clock in the morning? I was probably too young for the experience, but in any case, I kid you not, I was that kind of confused, slightly anxious child. I spent many troubled months wondering what Queen Elizabeth did with all those plums that were constantly posted to Buckingham palace by her obedient subjects. Send her Victorias? Why? Why on earth?

There were lots of problems. Dealing with the whole issue of friends was a constant worry, especially through the junior school years. Did they produce a big red post-box in the weeks leading up to Christmas when you were at school, Jeff? We had one. The idea was that you wrote Christmas cards for your friends while you were at home, then brought them to school the next day and posted them in the big red box. At the beginning of each morning some very fortunate boy would be assigned the role of postman. He was allowed to go round the four classrooms just after dinner delivering letters with great seriousness and pride. Those occasions twisted my insides up in a knot. Would there be any cards for me? If there weren't, what would I do with my face and my hands and my anguish? Would those to whom I had dared to send cards send me one on the same day, or, horror of horrors, would they, under pressure from their mothers, reluctantly bring a card for me on the following morning? How would I, how could I survive the face-reddening misery of 'pity post'?

Clothing caused another little pit of neurosis in my tender young soul. I had one older brother and one younger. Money was short, and you more or less dressed in whatever you could find. When you couldn't find anything for yourself, you were likely to have something far too large or far too small or far too ridiculously inappropriate imposed on you by a responsible adult.

'Well, I don't think you look silly,' my long-suffering mother would say desperately on a cold winter's morning as she enveloped all but my face and feet in some giant fisherman's pullover, 'and if they do say anything, *they're* the silly ones.'

'No mum,' I would explain with dispassionate resignation, 'they are not the silly ones. They are the ones who are wearing ordinary, normal clothes. I'm the silly one. I'm going to look like one of those things that crawl around on the bottom of the sea, only made of wool.'

I suppose it could have been worse. I might have had equally poor but far more eccentric parents who declared cheerfully, 'Tell you what! Up in the attic I've got one of those old-fashioned deep-sea diving suits with a window in the helmet. That'll do you just for today, and if they say you look silly, well, they're the silly ones.'

'Thanks, mum, but I think I'll stick to the Japanese admiral's uniform I've been wearing since Monday. I think they're getting used to that.'

'Sorry, love. Your big brother bagged that before breakfast. I'll just nip up to the attic. Won't be a mo. You be helping your little brother on with his clown shoes. . .'

One day I went to school with no pants on (underwear to you, Jeff). I often had no pants on (why am I writing about this?), but it didn't usually matter because our class never changed for anything. On this day we had to, and I knew someone would comment. They did.

'You forgot to put your pants on!' chirruped Alan who was changing behind me.

I gratefully accepted the assumption of forgetfulness, unconvincingly role-playing absent-mindedness with much head-shaking, tongue-clicking and fake laughter. Beetroot! I swear my whole head must have looked like one big beetroot. I wished I could spontaneously combust. Bits of charred purple everywhere.

One other memory: I'm sitting in Mr Cork's class. Yes, you read that correctly. Mr Cork. Mr Cork introduces a man connected with the local churches who has come to give a talk to our class. After giving his address the man is interested to know which of the boys who are present attend the local Sunday Schools. Each time he mentions the name of a church in the area around our village, one or more of my classmates lifts a hand. Suddenly I am filled with panic. I don't go to a Sunday School. I go to the local Roman Catholic church, often dressed in a long black mackintosh with a bare top underneath. They don't have a Sunday School there. If I am revealed to be a boy who doesn't go to Sunday School like all the others, I shall – well, I shall just die. I know I shall.

I swiftly develop a strategy. When the man says the name of a church and nobody lifts a hand, I'll put mine up. That'll be fine. There! He's just asked if anyone goes to St Mark's, wherever that is, and no-one's put their hand up. I shoot mine into the air, supporting my shoulder with one hand under my armpit and wildly waving to signify that I am comfortably one of the tribe. Oh, God! Another boy has put his hand up. Derek has put his hand up! He throws me an indignant glance and snorts with exasperation and scorn.

'*You* don't go to St Mark's! Why've you put your hand up?'

The demons gather around me in a dribbling pack, cackling and pointing. There's only one pathetically thin way out of this.

'Not *that* St Mark's!' I shout far too loudly. 'The *other* St Mark's. I go to the other St Mark's, not the one you go to, Derek. I go to a *different* St Mark's.'

Derek stares for a moment, and then his lip slowly curls. He knows.

I once tried to write a poem about this part of my life, the 'knitted-brow years' as I describe them to myself. This is how it went.

When I was a small boy in a small school,
With endless legs
And ears that widely proclaimed a head full of emergencies,
When I clung by bleeding fingertips
To thirty-three plus nine,
And cognitive dissonance was just a hard sum,
There were only two crimes.
The first was shouting in the corridors,
The second was to be a fool,
And when the bell,
The blessed bell,
Let me fling my body home,

I thought I might, at least, one day, aspire to rule in hell,
But now, I never hear the bell,
And part of me
Will always be
A fool
Screaming, in some sacred corridor.[3]

That rather pessimistic forecast is, thank God, considerably out of date now, but elements of it will always be part of me. I do quite a lot of shouting in sacred corridors these days, and will continue to do so as long as it's helpful. As for the rest of it, I will never lose my sympathy for and identification with anyone who doesn't think they fit, and lives on the cusp of feeling a fool. There's lots of us around, Jeff.

The liturgy you share with your mum is truly wonderful. Maybe that act alone will get you a bye into heaven. Jesus was keen on his mum.

Lots of everything,
Adrian

THIRTY

Dear Adrian,

I can completely identify with your memories of school. I look back and wish mine were more like *Billy Bunter* (although I wouldn't want to be the cake-obsessed character myself) or even *Tom Brown's Schooldays* (without all those prefects lining up boys to give them a good thrashing, which always seemed a bit suspect to me). Neither one of those series create an idyllic picture of schooldays, but they would be better than moments in my early education, that were more *Lord of the Flies*. William Golding described the piranha-like capacity of small boys well, don't you think? I too remember the red Christmas card postbox, and the fear and loathing it created. Happy Christmas? Not when you're thinking of signing up for someone's Lonely Hearts Club Band . . .

Allow me to reflect on one of my worst days – and this was at the hands of teachers, not fellow students. The episode is so pungently awful (in more ways than one) and I'll try to describe it all as delicately as I can, for fear of nauseating you and any of our readers.

It happened in infant school, where nervous small boys who are missing their mothers sometimes have accidents, if you get my drift, and I'm not talking about a pile-up on the M25. Someone in our class had rather obviously had such an accident; let's just say that it was apparent to all, and the 32 small children in the class were all looking around like the bewildered disciples at the Last Supper. They were seeking a traitor, whereas our class was on the hunt for a pooper.

The irate teacher stood at the front of the class, hands on hips, appalled expression on her face. She told us in no uncertain terms that unless someone owned up, she would have to resort to extreme measures. The silence was deafening.

And so the teacher had us all stand up at our desks, while she toured the class – and I can't believe that she did it and I'm writing about it – and patted each of our bottoms to identify the offender who was carrying excess weight. Finally, the culprit was found, and spent five harrowing minutes being utterly shamed before the assembled 32. I can hear the question in your mind, Adrian. Was I the vile offender? I'll let you decide . . .

Allow me to comment on your recent observation that you and I use humour, because it's one of the few ways to deal with all the darkness. And then you bravely talked of how you felt able to say something on behalf of God to Bob. I wonder if I could bring the two together – humour and talking for God – and tell you how I came to be at home with knowing that there are some Christians out there who happily write me off as a Bible carrying buffoon.

You asked me to make you and God laugh, Adrian. For quite a few years, I thought that it was easy to bring a smile to the Plass features, but to actually cause a giggle in the heart of God? That seemed totally impossible, about as likely as the comb-over becoming a fashionable hairstyle again, or Simon Cowell becoming a grief counsellor. In short, I didn't think God laughed, Adrian (except perhaps in sneering derision), and therefore logic demanded that, if I wanted to be like God, then I should pack laughter away into a trunk, shove it up in the loft, and shut the rickety hatch for good.

Some ancient Christians, eager to punish the flesh, used to wear hair shirts. I choose a corset, Adrian. I blush as I stand before you, naked and ashamed, in this admission, but I want to share the pain. Corsets are awkward, punishing contraptions, all whalebone constriction and taut ribbons and bows. Oh, did I mention that this was an emotional corset, Adrian? Surely I didn't give you the impression that I once had a penchant for ladies' underwear? No, my weakness for ping-pong was perversion enough . . .

The emotional corset that I wore was entirely of my own making, constructed from the notion that smiling wasn't for Christians. I'm not really sure where I developed this, because the minister of the church where I became a Christian was a hilarious chap called Brian, so I certainly didn't catch my emotional frigidity from him. I think that it came from an overdose of the idea that Christianity was about sacrifice, pain, and death, as well as purpose, joy and peace. I think if self-flagellation had been in vogue, as it was in darker days, then I would have bought a whip, and not just for the purposes of dodgy entertainment.

I decided that a furrowed brow was the most appropriate expression for a bright (make that dull) young Christian thing like myself. I actually went forward following a sermon at the end of a service, knelt down, and repented for feeling happy, Adrian. Even as I write this now, I'm a little angry still that I squandered my youth on this brand of spiritual constipation.

I don't know how I started to use humour, but it must have finally broken through the hard crust of my new found religion, like a wildflower emerging triumphant through concrete. Before becoming a Christian, I'd realised that I could occasionally say things in a way that made people smile, although I was never a great lover of jokes, or terribly good at telling them.

Sharing a joke is a thoroughly risky business, especially when one prefaces the joke by announcing, 'Oh, let me tell you a really funny gag!' It's always better to allow one's listeners to decide whether the joke is funny or not. But the telling of a joke (even without the suicidal opener) brings with it the potentially awful, potentially wonderful moment of the punch line, where you have to put all your cards and your cash. You show your hand, and hope to win a smile. But if you mess up the timing of the punch line (or even worse, forget it, as happened to a friend of mine who told a joke to a crowd of thousands at an event in Trafalgar Square), then, to use a term based on an ancient Greek word, you're stuffed.

Anyway, I began to realise that I could make people laugh, and frankly, for a while, I didn't like it. Silly pride meant that I wanted people to perceive me as a serious, scholarly, thoughtful soul, a person who could make weighty and memorable statements worth recording for posterity, even while ordering pizza.

You talked about talking on behalf of God, Adrian. Well, two people from different parts of the planet decided to give that a try, with wonderful results. They told me that God thought I was funny (what a terrifying thing to write; how absurd and pompous sounding. I can imagine one of our readers saying 'I don't think you are, Lucas, and now you've gone ahead and used the God of the Universe as expert witness to defend your daftness.' I truly hesitate to share this, at the risk of being very mis-understood). I have written about this elsewhere, but it was so life-changing, it bears repeating.

The first brave soul was in California. I had preached at a conference, and afterwards, a disarmingly attractive lady came up to me and whispered that she had 'seen a picture' and felt she had something to tell me from God. I braced myself for what I confess I anticipated being well-meaning twaddle. Forgive me, but I've got quite a collection, having been to some churches where they have more pictures than the Tate Gallery.

'When you were preaching tonight, I saw Jesus', she smiled, all warmth and sincerity and Californian perfect molars.

Bemused still, I enquired: 'Really? You saw Jesus? What was he doing?' Again Adrian, in defense of my cynicism, I've had too many experiences of best-intentioned people sharing banalities on behalf of God, as if he delights in cheering people up with little candy-coated nuggets of promise.

Unperturbed, she continued. 'He was laughing, Jeff. And he was clapping, and dancing. Jesus thinks you're really funny, Jeff. He enjoys what you do.'

I was initially stunned, but later collected my composure and promptly decided that she was kind, genuine, but over-enthusiastic. What is it about us, Adrian, that insulates us from the possibility of receiving some good or great news from God? If he announced to us that he was going to broadcast some of our nasty little sins, we'd sit up, because instinctively most of us expect rebuke. You mentioned our evangelical tendency to wallow waist-deep in guilt. I think you're right.

So I went to Los Angeles airport, and flew to Scotland, to speak at a boisterous Christian event that included a ceilidh, which was incredible fun, but also featured some of the sweatiest men and women that I have ever met. It was overwhelming . . .

I digress yet again.

Speaking at the Scottish conference one night, and having made no reference to the 'happening' in California, I was approached by a reserved-looking Presbyterian minister's wife.

'I saw a picture tonight, and I think I have something that God wants you to know,' she hissed a little furtively, as if she was trying to set me up with a spliff behind the bike sheds. 'But I need to share it privately, outside, and it includes me doing a mime.'

Horrors. Yikes.

A mime?

Now I was worried.

Outside, she shared her picture: a wonderful, fabulous repeat.

'I saw Jesus while you were speaking, Jeff. He was laughing, clapping, because he thinks you're really funny.'

And then came the mime. She reached her hand out to me, and placed her palm on my forehead, and acted as if she were soothing my brow. 'God wants to sooth your brow with this news, Jeff.'

Double yikes. Three explosions were taking place in my mind. First off, what if someone from the conference stepped out at that moment and spotted me and her in the shadows, having this little magic moment? 'Don't worry, it's just a prophetic mime' would sound like a lame excuse.

Secondly, the purist in me wanted to say, 'It's not a mime, because you've done some talking!'

And thirdly, I was bowled over by the grace of a God who would say, 'I like you when you laugh, and help others to do so.'

It was the day I stepped out of my corset.
And I'm glad I did.
Ever worn corsets, Adrian?
        Much love,
                Jeff

THIRTY-ONE

Hello again, Jeff.

Have I ever worn a corset? Possibly a couple of metaphorical ones, but my clearest memory of such horrors is connected with an experience that I endured while under the control of my Great Aunt Mab. Don't worry, this is not a tale of deliberate abuse. Great Aunt Mab certainly wasn't like that. She was the staunchest of staunch Methodists, a Christian with principles like iron girders. Having said that, you are about to hear about something so potentially scarring for a 4-year-old, that it's a wonder I've ended up such a serene and balanced individual.

Corsets. Do you know, just writing the word brings these hellish memories to the forefront of my mind. This is what happened. My Great Aunt Mab divested herself of her corsets in front of me when I was a small innocent child. Those are the bare facts. Oh dear . . .

I had been sent away for some mistily gynaecological reason to stay with Great Aunt Mab in Bromley. I can't remember who accompanied me on the Greenline bus from Tunbridge Wells to Bromley, but I do know that I was delivered to a shoe shop in Bromley High Street, the place where Auntie Mab worked. A couple of hours later we arrived at her house, where I was to spend the night.

Auntie Mab led me into the hall, stood me outside the toilet, and asked me if I wanted number one or number two. These were terms we never used in our house, so I considered for a moment, and opted for number one, hoping that it might be a cake. It wasn't.

It was bad enough being pushed into the toilet for no reason that I could fathom, but what followed was infinitely more disturbing. Auntie Mab took me to her bedroom and seemed to temporarily forget my existence. People who assume that 4-year-olds don't notice things are completely wrong. They do. I did.

Auntie Mab's flowered dress hit the floor, and a vast and terrifying salmon-pink apparatus was revealed, hung with buckles and straps and elasticated thingamabobs. My infant brain was stunned. What in the name of everything I understood was this ghastly piece of sartorial engineering, and why was my Methodist relative encased in it?

Moments later it happened. The pink monstrosity was released with a sound like the release of a giant catapult, and the essential Great Aunt Mab seemed to swell in front of my eyes until she was half as big again as she had been before. I was rooted to the spot, filled with a nameless dread of other terrible sights that might be awaiting me as the years passed.

My childhood was at an end.

Metaphorical corsets? Those who have been brave enough to listen to me bleating publicly more than once cannot fail to be aware that I think it very dangerous for us would-be followers of Jesus to stuff our real feelings away inside a corset of principles. Or indeed to corset ourselves into any moral contraption whose purpose is to make us harmlessly good, and safely prevent us from the dangerous business of doing what we see the Father doing. Those corsets are useless. They will burst in the end, and a jolly good job too.

I truly believe, Jeff, that we cannot serve God if mechanisms of worldly virtue are keeping the ingenuity and inventive power of the Holy Spirit at arm's length. No, if I want to be part of the Great Commission I need to be strong in areas that are unconfined and truly essential. Kindness. Respect for individuals. Listening as well as talking. Sticking with the principles that don't need a corset. Holding my nerve when things get tough. Listening and watching carefully to know when to gladly put aside my own agenda, so that I can allow the flexibility of Jesus to work through me.

This is no small thing. Flexibility is about being prepared to completely change direction if necessary. Here is an example that I love.

Saint Francis of Assisi was woken in the middle of the night once by the sound of crying. It turned out to be a brother who was faint with hunger. The rule of poverty was extremely strict in the Franciscan order, and food was scarce. What did Francis do? He collected together all the food that they had and they ate the lot, every scrap, in the middle of the night. In the morning the rule of poverty continued as before. Brilliant. Jesus-like. Francis of Assisi didn't need a corset. He was inflexible about that, but ready to be flexible about everything else. And that, I think, is what it takes.

Were there other points you wanted to make about ladies' underwear, Jeff, or have we covered it? If there is something else you really need to talk about – don't hold it in.

Cheers,

Adrian

THIRTY-TWO

Dear Adrian,

I am afraid that my mind is now damaged irreparably. Your vivid description of Aunt Mab, tumbling from the confines of her corset in all of her bosomy enormity, is now etched on my mind, and has prompted a painful memory of my own. I'm thankful that you were not suffocated by that sudden bursting dam of flesh, and that you have obviously experienced some healing from the experience. After all, you grew up, got married and had children, so at least you didn't develop a horror for the female form.

I was having lunch with a minister and his family, and they had a relative visiting them for a few days. This lady was not just well endowed. Quite simply, she had the most enormous breasts that I have ever seen, and made Dolly Parton look like Twiggy. Now I know that inordinate breast size can be a very real issue, and I don't want to offend any of our female readers by making light of what can be a heartbreaking business. The comments that follow are not directed in any derisory way at her, but rather at me as I struggled to see past her most obvious presenting feature.

We sat around the lunch table, and it quickly occurred to me that this dear woman had probably endured stares for most of her adult life. So I scribbled an internal note to self, and determined not to join the crowd of gawkers. Isn't it difficult not to stare when you've made a decision not to stare? Those gigantic bosoms seemed to magnetically draw the eye, like a moth to a light.

Anyway, I managed to maintain a rigidly fixed eye contact with her that was so intense, she probably thought I had a side job working as a military interrogator.

Lunch was pleasant enough, except for a tense moment (for me) when we were talking about workplace politics. The lady said that her employer was quite secretive, and it created uncertainty in the office.

I nodded, still wondering if she was actually wearing mobile scaffolding. 'Yes, I know', I said, 'It can be very difficult working with people who like to keep their cards close to their . . . er, ah, (I broke into a sweat), close to their . . .'

'Chest', she said, so sweetly. She was kind enough to completely ignore my Freudian hesitation.

All of which takes me back to our earlier conversation about how we all want to be noticed. We all want to be seen – but we want people to see us, not our most obvious 'unusual' feature, be it eyebrows that join in the middle, breasts that arrive at a destination five seconds ahead of the rest of one's body or, in my case, a broken nose that can sniff around corners. When the nurse tells the duty doctor in the Accident and Emergency department, 'There's a colon cancer in cubicle B, and a fractured jaw in C, doctor', the real casualty is personhood. And yet how easy it is to categorise people, and if we do notice them at all, it's with just a cursory glance, one that diminishes them. We end up not seeing them at all, but only that which is screamingly obvious about them.

The other thought that was prompted by Aunt Mab divesting herself of her garments in front of a traumatised 4-year-old is that God's provision of designer fig leaves in the garden was a pretty nifty idea, don't you think? Not only do our clothes help us avoid hypothermia, but they wonderfully disguise the truth about almost everybody: with the exception of a small club of the stunningly beautiful, nakedness is generally ugly. Even the beautiful brigade is helped along by airbrushing. Remember my unfortunate experience at the nudist beach, and my nervousness about hot dogs ever since? Fig leaves were a brilliant idea.

I think that's one of the reasons I enjoy our letters. We both, in our different ways, try to 'bleat publicly', to use your delightful metaphor, about the truth. We take pleasure in interrogating clichés and debunking slogans. More valuably, we try to wear our hearts on our sleeves, as far as one can do without causing the heart to stop altogether.

I'm in one of those accountability groups that are in vogue, and I'm glad and grateful to be part of it. The four of us have developed authentic friendships that grow when they're fertilised by shared laughter and tears, and we've walked through some harrowing circumstances together. But one of the best conversations we've had was a recent discussion about whether we're fooling ourselves, as we call ourselves an accountability group. We wrestled with the question – could we live what's on the label, and actually be accountable? If any one of us did something seismically sinful (if sin can be measured like earthquakes), that could cost us our marriages, our livelihoods, our friendships – would we actually take the risk and tell? The danger of being in a group so called is that it can be self-deceiving. Yes, I'm accountable, because I'm in an accountability group. It is rather like believing that we are fit because we carry a gym membership card in our wallet.

Even if we want to take the risk and share our struggles, there are still challenges to overcome. My problem is that I'd quite like deeply trusted friends to really know me, but I sometimes wonder if *I* really know me, and I'm the one charged with the responsibility of introducing – myself. We've talked about planetariums. I wish I could visit an Innertarium, where instead of gazing out there, I could peer inside me and make sense of the labyrinth of motives, emotions, hopes, dreams, frailties, fears and a host of other flotsam that is drifting around in the inner space that is me.

I know that you've said, when asked to confess a sin, you like to have a fairly neutral sin ready to share – a minor tax evasion, if I remember rightly. I've been through those times too, when I've been tempted to tearfully confess that I've been lax with my harp practice (so lax that I've never actually owned or played one) or better still, admit to a sin that actually makes me look quite good, like saying I felt a twinge of pride when I gave that staggeringly generous cheque in the offering last week.

So where do you feel safe, Adrian? Anywhere?

Last thing: earlier you mentioned 'holding your nerve'. I've heard you talk about that before. Wasn't that what you said when you and Bridget were involved in a nasty car accident? The thing is this: I'm staggering through a couple of difficult situations right now. I'd really like to hold my nerve, but I'm tempted to leap around like Corporal Jones in *Dad's Army*, and utterly panic, while, of course, telling everybody else not to panic.

So any chance of a few hints on nerve-holding?

Much love,
Jeff

THIRTY-THREE

Dear Jeff,

The problem with writing, or responding to writing about breasts is that a sort of automatic pun-fest switches itself on and refuses to switch itself off. Nevertheless, I shall start my next sentence as I had intended to begin this letter, and we'll just have to go from there.

A couple of things occur to me as I read about your eye-popping dinner experience. One is the memory of a lady called Mrs Breen who was the headmistress at one of the junior schools that my children attended. Mrs Breen had total control, not only over the children in her care, but over the entire staff and all the parents as well. I remember asking myself what it was about Mrs Breen that allowed her to gain such power over so many other people. She was quite short in stature, her voice was not particularly commanding and, as far as I can recall, she never had anything very interesting to say. And yet, she held us all, young and old, male and female, in her thrall with apparent ease. She could have run four or five of those small African republics at the same time without raising her voice, and with no danger whatsoever of rebellion or even mild disagreement. How did she do it?

In the end I think I identified the source of her power. It was twofold, and these twin elements of domination worked together to awesome effect.

The first was her eye. When Mrs Breen fixed you with her unwavering eye you experienced an irrational but overwhelming sense of some great arsenal of deadly weapons, primed and ready for use, stored in the imponderable cavity behind those two boiled gooseberry orbs. On the first and only occasion that I decided to express a minor objection to some aspect of school practice, I opened my mouth to speak to Mrs Breen and shut it almost immediately. The eyes were just too much for me. I didn't give up, though. Aware that any words I tried to say whilst under that double-barrelled gooseberry threat would sour and die before they had a chance to emerge, I dropped my own eyes to escape the pressure, and it was then that I encountered this formidable lady's second tier of attack.

Have you noticed in the course of your life, Jeff, how something that has a very distinct effect in one context, can have a completely different, even opposite effect in another? Mrs Breen's bust was a case in point, and I use the term 'bust' very deliberately, because it allows us to move seamlessly out of the world of male fantasy, and into a world of strange, nameless dread. There is enough unhappiness in this weary world without Mrs Breen's bust, a jutting outcrop of insurmountable defence, which somehow brought to mind all the little disappointments and failed dreams of my past. The world seemed darker, if I can put it like that.

It was back to the gooseberries thereafter, and back to the inevitable nodding, puppet-like acquiescence to everything that the headmistress said or suggested. There was nowhere else for my eyes to go. Gooseberries or bust. I may be the first person ever to write that last sentence.

By the way, I once wrote a little piece of doggerel that attempted to sum up the uncrossable contextual mammary chasm that I mentioned earlier. One couplet went like this:

That kind of wide and spreading bust,
Attracts respect, but never lust.

Not exactly Shakespeare, but it does encapsulate one of the great verities of human experience, don't you think?

Another thought was triggered by your very understandable struggle to see past that lady's most obvious presenting feature. It reminded me of an unforgettable moment when, in our very early twenties, Bridget and I were introduced by a couple we knew to their elderly parents. Said elderly parents had their backs to us as the introduction began, and they turned to face us as it was completed.

The man was wearing a plastic nose.

It wasn't quite skin colour, Jeff. It was pinker than that. Just a hint of, well – circus, if you know what I mean. I didn't know what to do. For one moment I thought perhaps this venerable gentleman might be a bit of a trickster, a jovial old character who loved to shock and amuse in his own small way. I came very close to pointing at the pink proboscis and forcing myself to chortle appreciatively, but as no one else was reacting to the bizarre sight in any way, I restrained myself.

In the course of our conversation nobody referred to the false nose at all, but what a strain! Talk about the elephant in the room. A frenzied idiot inside me wanted to burst out with: 'Anyway, never mind all that – tell us about your nose. Tell us about your nose that isn't real. Tell us about the fake pink nose that I can't keep my eyes off. Tell me, tell me, tell me why you're wearing it, or I shall punch you on the er . . .'

Later we learned that the poor old chap had needed serious surgery on his nose, and the false appliance was covering up the healing process. They should have warned us, though, shouldn't they?

A serious point arising from this is summed up by a game that I used to play with my friend John Hall. It was called 'Cumulonimbus'. This is how it was played. In front of us on the table we would place an encyclopaedia open at the double page where cloud formations were listed and illustrated. I might start by reading the name of one of the cloud formations out loud, then John would read another, and so on. Cirrocumulus, Cirrus, Altostratus, Nimbostratus, on and on we would go until one of us said 'Cumulonimbus'. The first one to say that was the winner. Got it? Insane? Well, yes, perhaps, but the really interesting part of the game occurred when we invited somebody else to play the game with us, and John and I explained the rules with deadly seriousness.

'Sorry – are you saying that, to win, all you have to do is say "Cumulonimbus"?'

That was the usual question from a newcomer after hearing the 'rules'.

'Yes,' we'd reply. 'Wow! You've picked it up very quickly. Well done!'

Actually playing the game with visitors revealed that, broadly speaking, there are two kinds of people in this world. The first sort snorted derisively and simply said 'Cumulonimbus' as soon as it was their turn. John and I would shake our heads in awe, amazed by their brilliance.

'Not much point playing against you,' we'd say despairingly. 'You're a natural.'

Others would catch on immediately, and perhaps try a tentative 'Nimbostratus'.

'Ah,' we'd respond appreciatively, pleased to find one more person as foolish as us on the planet, 'see where you're going with that – I think you're going to be good at this . . .'

The serious point arising from this is the fact that many heated discussions and arguments can be won by simply referring to a very personal and usually irrelevant aspect of one's opponent that cannot be denied and is as effective in conflict as a blow from a baseball bat.

'Anyway, you had an affair twelve years ago, so your views on the euro don't count for much, do they?'

'How do you square your absurd contention that Roman Catholics are not real Christians with that unpleasant mole on your chin?'

Silly examples, but they are not a million miles from the truth, unfortunately.

Finally Jeff, you talked about the true value of your accountability group and the question of how you or I can continue to hold our nerve when the pressure is on big-time.

Only last night, I wrote this foolish little rhyme in my head as I was waiting for sleep to not come. I don't know about you, but every now and then I catch a clear if fleeting glimpse of my own absurdity and shortcomings. This used to depress me, and it still does a bit, but not nearly as much. This was the rhyme:

I have a problem with myself,
And here's the crux of it,
However hard I try to change,
I'm such a pompous git.

I know that I can be selfish, arrogant, mouthy, thought-less, jealous, faithless, disloyal – you can finish the list, Jeff. I don't suppose we're that different. However, the awareness that has been growing in me increasingly over the last two or three years is that Jesus (if he exists) is more than a little bored by my obsession with me, my sins, my virtues, my progress, my weaknesses, my strengths, my self-examination and the way in which all these things distract me from getting on with the job.

Perhaps he says to both of us, 'Look, if you were in a boat, and you suddenly saw me on the shore, would you jump in the water – sins and complications and all – and run as fast as you could towards me, simply because you love me? Would you sit beside the fire with me, share a bit of fish, and make a decision that you'll go and love peo-ple for me even though you are a grade one pillock? I don't expect you to be perfect, I want you to be obedient. Whose side are you on? Yours – or yours and mine?'

For me, that's the most important accountability group of all, but then, I'm not a very good joiner.

Somehow, Jeff, I've got to become less obsessed by my sins and my faith than he is, and it's not easy. Less bur-densome in the end, though, I would guess. What do you think?

> Lots of love,
> Adrian

THIRTY-FOUR

Dear Adrian,

Let me describe for you the effect your last letter had on me. I'll use just one word. It was devastating. Panic not, Captain Mainwaring. Devastating is a word that conjures up images of a fat concrete wrecking ball, swung by a towering demolition crane, slowly, methodically pummelling a building, finally reducing it to a dust-shrouded pile of bricks.

Devastation is a word that's being yelled by panicked families around here right now. I mentioned earlier that a terrible forest fire is raging in Northern Colorado. One lady has died locally, trapped within a circle of flame that literally sucked all oxygen out of the air. Along with the refuges that we call home, so many artefacts and souvenirs have been turned to ash in the two hundred feet high flames. I can see it in the distance, right now, as I look out of my study window. Devastation. Although I think your letter calls for some walls to crumble or a spark-scattering bonfire or two, it's potentially devastating in a wonderfully positive way. You wrote a book once called *Clearing Away the Rubbish*, didn't you? Sometimes demolition needs to happen in order to build something more beautiful, more substantial.

When you describe a Jesus who perhaps is bored with our constant self-evaluation, flittering around like we do taking endless stock checks on our progress and sins and strengths and weaknesses, something in me really, really wants to believe that you're right. And there's nothing casual about my hope that the Jesus you portray is the real Jesus. The thought of him being like that is like ice-cold water on the lips of a weary traveler, who has been seared by the Sahara. It's like an open door of freedom, an offer of pardon from Death Row.

I really don't want to be a manically self-obsessed, always checking, counting, measuring, and categorizing everything. I don't want to be a religious peacock, endlessly preening and picking and sometimes unable to resist flashing a rainbow display of plumage, as I strut around in my religious glad rags, my coat of many colours that announces that I'm favoured, blessed, and that I have a neat, disciplined, holy, pristine life. No, I certainly don't want that. That coat is a dyed straitjacket.

To respond to your question about whether you and I would get out of the boat if the stranger on the shore turned out to be Jesus, I know that the answer for both of us would be a resounding yes. Knowing us, we'd probably mess up the little trip from boat to beach, and stumble over the side and land on an oar, and think that we were in the warm shallows, only to discover that we're in freezing, twenty-feet-deep water. We'd flail around and cough and spit, and wonder why the hell no one had provided orange flotation devices, and finally drag ourselves up the beach, spluttering, where we'd throw ourselves down exhausted by the fire, and tell Jesus that it's a little early for fish – is anything else available? Porridge, or better still, an omelette? Even though our response to him would be characteristically messy, uncool, and might make him put down his fish skewer and lean back and laugh, I know we'd be there, Adrian. And I'd like to be bold enough to say that, yes, even with our Olympic-level capacity for being pillocks, to use your word, we'd want to love people for him, because I do believe that's what we're about, isn't it?

I think we agonise over life and faith and everything, not because there's nothing interesting on TV, or because we want to pick things apart just for the joy of picking, but because we hate to see so much pain in the church. How was it we began this book? You described the church as a battlefield, with wounds and tears and a wild yearning for home.

I so want you to be right about Christianity not being an endless, dull sin management system. I'm convinced that Jesus is certainly not picky. Looking at the gospels, especially Mark, who manages to portray the batty exploits of the disciples, it's obvious that Jesus could have spent every waking moment of his three years with them dissecting, probing, confronting, and evaluating who they were. Much of the time they'd have earned the red pen treatment that I remember from my school days: C+, could do better. But he didn't. They were invited into partnership and friendship, even though they were so good at blundering pomposity and missing the boat as well as getting out of it.

The challenge is, I really want to believe that Jesus is as you describe him, but there's so much that needs to be demolished in order for me to do it. Here's a stark fact: ever since I became a Christian at the age of 17, I have woken up too many times with a sense that C+ is written over my day before it's even begun. It's exhausting.

I sense a call to something better, an invitation to allow some of the thick walls of my Christianity to genuinely topple before grace. But when I hear that tantalizing invitation, 'Come to me, all you that are burdened and heavy laden, and I'll give you rest', I want to send a RSVP, but then, at times, sneer in the face of it. 'What do you mean, Jesus, your burden is easy, and your yoke is light? Not for me, it isn't! Oh no. Some of my best days have been blighted by a sense that whatever I do, whoever I become, you'll still be drumming your fingers on some great desk somewhere, poised to mark down my life with your big red pen. Nothing light or easy about that, eh?'

Perhaps our earlier conversations about death and eternity have some relevance here, because, for me, some of this is about how I feel – or fear – it's all going to work out in the end. When I die, or when Jesus returns (in whatever way that works), it's then that all our yearnings and hopes and dreams and fears will be realised – or shattered.

At the risk of sounding like I need serious therapy, let me share a recurring dream that has flitted in and out of my night times throughout my life. In my dream, actually nightmare, it is very late, probably after midnight, and I am trying to get home. I am standing on an Underground station somewhere in London, and it is deserted. Suddenly two things happen: I hear the faraway rumble of the approaching train, still deep in the tunnel. At that moment I hear the sound of footsteps echoing from the other end of the platform, as a stranger walks down the steps. The train suddenly emerges from the tunnel, all noise and lights, and the stranger looks at me, and then howls with laughter; the cavernous station fills with the terrifying sound of cruel, heartless cackling. At that moment, the platform tips up and becomes a slippery slope, and I frantically hold onto a bench, to a cigarette machine, desperate to avoid sliding down into the pathway of the train that is now just feet away.

I don't for a moment think that the sneering person in the dream is Jesus, but the truth is that much of the time I approach him as if he is.

So it seems to me that the core question, 'Who is Jesus?' is the one that we've got to keep asking. We've got to tread carefully as we do, because like the disciples, I want to manage him, and choreograph his movements, but even go further than that. Sometimes I'm tempted to try to make him in my own image. I want to pick up an airbrush and amend him, edit him, tame him, make him someone that I can live with, and not just live for.

I mentioned the fire. Right now, there's a thin layer of soot on my car. Actually, it is on everything. It reminds me of Bonhoeffer's famous statement that the church's main mission is to wash the face of Jesus, to remove the religious grime so that his true, irresistible face will be seen. This is not just about us, is it? If the Jesus that we know looks like a chimney sweep, then that's the Jesus we'll tend to introduce to others.

All of this is terrifying. Whenever we wilfully begin to demolish something we've become accustomed to, we can wonder what we'll have left over at the end. Will anything useful or beautiful be left standing, or will we be left in the middle of a barren building site, all mud pools and scaffolding, planks and discarded buckets, and nothing much else?

But it's the core question. Who are you, Jesus? What are you like? I'd love to have that breakfast with Jesus, and I'd like you to be there, Adrian, not only because I think it'd be incredibly entertaining, but I could also blame you if I'd got things horribly wrong. It was his fault, Lord.

One last thing, Adrian, which may have everything or nothing to do with this conversation. Yesterday, we spent some time in church offering a very specific request.

Thousands of fire fighters are working twenty-four-hour shifts, toiling in weather of 104 degrees (in old money) – and they also have to deal with the furnace heat of the fire and their stiflingly heavy protective uniforms. Clear blue skies and blazing sunshine was the order of the day yesterday, with no change forecasted on the horizon.

So we did something very silly yesterday morning at church. Even as we prayed, we confessed the silliness of it. We prayed that it would rain. We didn't declare with loud, certain voices that it would, but we asked for rain.

And do you know what, Adrian? Yesterday evening, literally out of the blue, huge black rain clouds marched towards the site of the fire. The news reports are just saying that the fire crews stood and cheered when they felt the rainfall on their faces, and saw it falling on the flames.

The fire still burns, Adrian. But it rained.

Honestly, it did.

> With love,
> Jeff

PS: I wanted to ask you quickly about your insane game of Cumulonimbus. I'm very intrigued by it, and can't work out whether you and John Hall should share a room in a secure facility, or whether this is in fact a genius of an idea.

The intriguing thing is, that according to the normal rules of life, the game would obviously be lost by the first person to have to resort to saying the aforementioned cloud, Cumulonimbus, simply because you'd run out of available cloud types to list, and so you'd finally concede defeat.

But in your game, the one who says this can win at any time. Does this mean that the true winner is really the one who admits he's a loser, and he triumphs and trumps the other person by running out of ideas?

If so, it sounds like a thoroughly Christian game to me.

But then of course, it might just be that you're both quite mad.

PPS: I've been thinking about your Mrs Breen, the gooseberry-eyed headmistress who could freeze conversation or criticism with just a stare. Your description of her brought a flush of shame. In my fledgling days as a Christian leader, I was battling a black hole of insecurity within (of course I'm totally secure now, *not* . . .). I was a pastor at the tender age of twenty-one. It's difficult to be a wise shepherd of the flock of God when you're still looking forward to shaving.

Looking back on it, it was ridiculous, although probably God's idea – perhaps the two can co-mingle. The very thought that I might proffer any scrap of wisdom to my congregation was absurd, and deep down they knew that, and so did I. For their part, they showed immeasurable kindness and patience. Even though I probably pelted them weekly with an assortment of clichés and slogans, they never took up stones in response.

But at times I was guilty of deflecting criticism, corralling anyone who thought outside of the box, and silencing innocent questions. I didn't have gooseberry eyes but I had other sneaky little devices, tried and tested weapons, guaranteed to derail anyone who might question my authority. One of the most effective weapons was caricature. Trish, a lady who was very rightly concerned about the lack of women in leadership in our church, and was also a duffel-coat-wearing social worker with a multi-coloured woolly scarf (much beloved by ex-hippies and people who spent the August Bank Holiday listening to rock bands while parked in muddy fields). With a nudge and a wink, I quickly managed to sideline her as being woolly in her theology as well as her neckwear, a slightly liberal trendy free spirit who just didn't understand the truth. It never occurred to me that she might be right, which she was. I have subsequently tracked her down, and thanked her for her patience.

Then there was always the 'You're being divisive' card. In some churches, perfectly valid but awkward questions are silenced with just one sentence: 'You are being divisive.' In fact, I found there was no shortage of weaponry to facilitate subtle and unsubtle leadership manipulation. Confronted with an uncomfortable issue, I could say that I'd pray about it. The more uncomfortable the issue, the less likely it was that I would actually pray about it. And I could use proof texts, often using verses wrenched out of context: no matter. This kind of warfare is more akin to laying a smokescreen than lobbing a grenade, but it usually does the trick. Another beauty was the 'I'm afraid you just don't understand, and when you're as spiritually mature as me, maybe you will' line, although it's incredible to think that I even tried this Gnostic stunt, especially as I had only recently navigated my way through puberty. You see, I had my own version of gooseberry eyes. Lots of leaders do.

With love again,

Jeff

THIRTY-FIVE

Greetings Jeff,

Yes, John and I were always rather good at being constructively bonkers, but I think the real winner of Cumulonimbus is the one who pours some more wine, proposes a toast to the spirit of levity, madness, common sense and love, and closes the encyclopaedia with a resounding thump!

This brings me back, by a slightly circuitous route, to your recent letter about the nature of Jesus. Many years ago I took a friend to visit Bishop Peter Ball in the Sussex village of Litlington where he lived. Peter and Bridget and I had been ripples in a pool of folk involved in a little local television programme called *Join the Company*, broadcast by TVS. This epilogue-style production was the last programme of the night in the days when 24-hour TV had not yet begun.

Bridget and I had loved our encounters with Peter. A TVS cameraman, not a Christian as far as I was aware, had once said to me, 'When I listen to that man speaking it's like sitting on the edge of a big, beautiful, peaceful lake.' And it was. Exactly like that.

My friend's Christian walk had been twisted and tortuous through many stages, and for long periods of his life. I wanted him to meet Peter, and, even more, I wanted him to catch a glimpse of the God in whom Peter seemed to take such an unusual delight. I was not disappointed. Nor was my friend. As we walked away from the house he said to me, 'You know what, Adrian, he knows a different God to the one I know. His God's nice!'

Later, these words chimed very sweetly with the truth that I was to understand myself as I clambered out of the deep, dark hole of stress and confusion in the mid-eighties, an experience that I have mentioned to you before. Actually, I'm sure you'll remember me saying the following words several times during our tours, Jeff, especially in the question and answer sessions in the second half of those evenings.

'It's going to sound rather unspectacular and possibly a bit trivial, but the most important thing I ever learned about being a Christian was very simple. God is nice, and he likes me.'

I encountered the heart of this shining revelation once more at Spring Harvest, when a man who has an alarmingly good track record for passing specific, non-fuzzy messages from the heart of God to the hearts of men and women said to me, 'I know what God thinks about you.'

Horrors! Did I want to hear the answer to a question that I had secretly been wanting to ask ever since I made a thin decision to follow Jesus when I was a useless 16-year-old? No, I did not. But I couldn't get away. I had to listen. I was terrified that, through this man, God would say, 'Look, I've read your books. I've been to almost half of one of your talks. Could you stop? Just stop. There's no great harm done so far. Just call it a day and we'll leave it there. Okay?'

'So err, what does he think of me?' I asked, with a slight tremor in my voice.

'He loves you without any condition at all,' said the man. 'He loves you whether you work for him or whether you don't. Whether you're good or whether you're bad. Whether you love him or whether you don't. He just loves you.'

My knees went weak, Jeff. I had been wanting to hear this for so many years. There had always seemed to be a forest of modern, subtle pharasaical arguments obscuring and blocking off the path that would take me to a place where I could believe and know at last that Grace, sweet Grace was not just a clever disguise for the usual game of earning and succeeding and failing and being dropped at the last minute because I hadn't made the grade, or because I had committed the ultimate sin of murder or excessive ping-pong or something even worse or better.

I certainly have not got where I need to be yet, but I'll tell you this, Jeff. I seriously think that I'm safer sitting on that beach with Jesus, eating fish and having a laugh and knowing I'm loved, than in many, many sections and enclaves of what we call the church, where so many brows are creased by worry about whether God loves them enough to put up with them in Paradise.

'Lord, remember me when you come to your Kingdom.'

'Sorry, mate, it's not that simple . . .'

Yes it is.

For two thousand years the Holy Spirit has been battling against the chronic tendency of misguided teachers and preachers to place extra burdens on us fragile Christians. He did it through Jesus: 'The Sabbath was made for man, not man for the Sabbath.' Through Paul: 'Put your knives away, it's circumcision of the heart that's needed.' Through the man who initiated the Sailors' Society after walking past a church on the south coast with a sign outside saying 'No Sailors or Prostitutes'. Through people like Paul Tournier in this age, who had the courage and the common sense to tell hurting Christians blazingly obvious truths, such as 'Your conversion really didn't do you any good at all.' Through idiots like you, who make people laugh and cry and begin to hope that God might care about them after all.

All of it, every last little passionate push by the Holy Spirit, is aimed at landing us, not in a swamp of questions and concerns and self-obsessed entrail examination, but on a little beach beside a beautiful lake where we can find peace with a friend who will undoubtedly have a job for us to do.

Here are my questions for you, Jeff, and I have to answer similar ones.

How many more people have to be sent to you with the message that God finds you funny and enjoys what you do, before you begin to believe it?

Jesus says, 'Come unto me all you who are weary and heavy-laden and I will give you rest.' If you haven't found rest, who have you been going to? Clearly not Jesus. Where is he, and who have you been talking to?

Would you really want to jump from that boat? Do you seriously want to be with the one who makes such ridiculous demands on you, and keeps a very meticulous record of all your fat sins and skinny virtues? Do you like him? Does he like you? Do you honestly want to splash your way hopefully to that man, only to be told off when you get there, and find there's not enough fish for two? Or will you stay in the boat, unwilling to take the risk, catching as many fish as you possibly can in the hope that when you reach 490 he'll call you in, give you a Blue Peter badge and send you out again?

Job got it right, didn't he? In the good old pre-boil days he spoke to the people on behalf of God. The Bible says his words were like the spring rain. Perhaps they extinguished fires of fear and disappointment. We also learn that when he smiled at them, 'they could scarcely believe it'. Imagine – God appears to be nice! How can that be? Nothing changes much, does it, Jeff?

God bless,

Adrian

Endnotes

1   Plass, A., *Silences and Nonsenses* (Milton Keynes: Authentic Media Limited, 2010).
2   Peterson, E.H., *The Message: The Bible in Contemporary Language* (Colorado Springs: NavPress, 2002).
3   Plass, A., *Silences and Nonsenses* (Milton Keynes: Authentic Media, 2010).

Seriously Funny

Life, Love and God . . .
Musings Between Two
Good Friends

Adrian Plass and
Jeff Lucas

Having delighted, amused and challenged thousands of readers around the world for many years with their individual titles, Adrian Plass and Jeff Lucas are now ready to let their readers in on their private correspondence. As Adrian says in his first letter, 'If we were pushed into a corner and forced to be absolutely straight about our religion, what kind of truth would emerge?'

This book is the answer to that question. It is a joy to read, funny, sad, controversial and, above all, honest.

978-1-85078-869-0

War of the Worlds

How to Avoid Leading a Double Life

Adrian Plass

There is a war going on in the Church, says Adrian Plass: a war between two worlds – one where honesty is valued, and one where it's shunned. That same war is going on inside every Christian with areas of conflict such as death, weakness, sacred cows, the Bible, prayer, commitment . . . all are covered in this book.

War of the Worlds goes to the heart of Christian life and once again Adrian skilfully employs humour to help us absorb his more profound points.

978-1-85078-956-7

Up Close & Personal

What Helen Did Next

Jeff Lucas

Helen Sloane, single and a social worker from Frenton-on-Sea, is struggling to rebuild her life after the murder of her father when she receives a new blow – her beloved church leaders leave. Aaron continually lets her down, James is engaged elsewhere . . . but then she meets a new man, a normal man, a wonderful man.

Has the tide turned for Helen Sloane? Will she learn the identity of her father's killer? Does hard case Hayley join the human race? Is the musical a surprise success or an embarrassing disaster? This is a heart-warming story, full of humour and insight.

978-1-85078-888-1

Authentic

We trust you enjoyed reading this book from Authentic Media. If you want to be informed of any new titles from this author and other exciting releases you can sign up to the Authentic newsletter online:

www.authenticmedia.co.uk

Contact us
By Post: Authentic Media
52 Presley Way
Crownhill
Milton Keynes
MK8 0ES

E-mail: info@authenticmedia.co.uk

Follow us: